SECRECY AND FIELDWORK

RICHARD G. MITCHELL, JR.
Oregon State University

Qualitative Research Methods
Volume 29

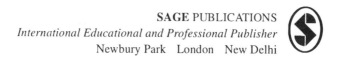

SAGE PUBLICATIONS
International Educational and Professional Publisher
Newbury Park   London   New Delhi

For information address:

SAGE Publications, Inc.
2455 Teller Road
Newbury Park, California 91320

SAGE Publications Ltd.
6 Bonhill Street
London EC2A 4PU
United Kingdom

SAGE Publications India Pvt. Ltd.
M-32 Market
Greater Kailash I
New Delhi 110 048 India

Printed in the United States of America

Library of Congress Cataloging-in-Publication Data

Mitchell, Richard G.
    Secrecy and fieldwork / Richard G. Mitchell, Jr.
        p.   cm. — (Qualitative research methods ; v. 29)
    Includes bibliographical references.
    ISBN 0-8039-4384-9 (cl.) — ISBN 0-8039-4385-7 (pb)
    1. Social sciences—Field work. 2. Confidential communications.
3. Secrecy. I. Title. II. Series.
H62.M533   1993
300'.723—dc20   93-25527

93 94 95 96   10 9 8 7 6 5 4 3 2 1

Sage Production Editor: Judith L. Hunter

CONTENTS

For Richard G. Mitchell, Sr.,
who shared so many of life's secrets with his son.

EDITORS' INTRODUCTION

To be accused of being deceitful, manipulative, or otherwise less than up front about fieldwork purposes and methods is a qualitative researcher's nightmare. Any ethnographer so morally discredited is bound to find opportunities to continue inquiry jeopardized, not to mention collegial and institutional audiences distanced. With the risks of ruptured rapport so substantial, it is little wonder that fieldworkers are prone to stress the importance of developing and nurturing professional relationships between themselves and their subjects.

Yet, even in this, we can never be totally honest. With the best of intentions, we frequently discover that we are being linked with images and backgrounds we cannot hope to maintain. The field identities that mark us are, after all is said and done, often of our own manufacture. The impressions we project—indeed, sometimes market—are only partially under our own management. Like it or not, we are no different from anyone else. We are secretive, and we selectively conceal and reveal.

Richard G. Mitchell, Jr., takes as a departure point in Volume 29 of the Sage Qualitative Research Methods Series the proposition that secrecy is omnipresent in social action. The rub of the secret side of ethnography is that even as we may ignore or mask our secrets they continue to influence the quality of access we have to people and cultural systems and shape what we are positioned to learn. Needless to say, the secret lives of those we study are similarly structured.

Secrecy and Fieldwork pulls no punches in examining the distribution and nature of secrecy in society. Mitchell frames his treatment in symbolic interactionism, pointing out that secrets as denied knowledge contrast with ignorance (absent knowledge) and mysteries (inaccessible knowledge). Strategic secrets may be partitioned into altruistic, egoistic, and normative kinds. Tactical secrets have ethnocentric, egocentric, and resource-focused variants. In Mitchell's view, the key to successful fieldwork entails special awareness of how all social actors, researchers included, choreograph concealment and disclosure.

Fieldwork roles, whether these are selected by qualitative researchers or imposed by subjects, foster expectations about what the ethnographer should know and feel. Mitchell usefully expands on this theme with a four-cell grid characterizing researcher roles as either "naive" or "informed"

about the cultural and political setting, and as "supportive" or "unsuppor-
tive" of local values and agendas. Drawing vivid examples from the field
reports of others as well as from his own covert work with survivalists,
he identifies the problems secrecy creates for each role.
The ambivalence people experience about secrecy extends well into the
intellectual realm. Mitchell is provocative in describing a mainstream
liberal camp in American sociology opposed to covert research (although
the record of unfortunate consequences attributable to such endeavors is
very short) and dedicated to the promulgation of codes of professional ethics
and informed consent standards. A rival humanist community challenges
this orthodoxy, illustrating that ethical problems in sociological work are
more than matters of the misuse of methods and can entail the victimization of entire social classes. Mitchell advises independent researchers
operating in this milieu to prepare well for questions about their technical
competence, the benefits that would accrue to people studied, and the
likely impact of research on social order.
This book is a wake-up call and an important addition to the Qualitative
Research Methods Series. It compels us to consider a small spin on a well-
known conclusion—secrecy is too important to be left to the methodologists.

—Marc L. Miller
Peter K. Manning
John Van Maanen

ACKNOWLEDGMENTS

Thanks to Dean Dorn, John Galliher, Daniel Glaser, Bob Prus, Gideon Sjoberg, Gary Tiedeman and the editors of this series for the suggestions and encouragements they offered. Chris Pyle's patience in bringing the manuscript into readable form deserves special mention. Thanks, too, to the anonymous survivalists among whom I learned some of the challenges of covert research and to colleague Eleen Baumann who shared in many of these adventures. Opportunity to examine the American Sociological Association's archived records was made possible by permission of ASA and by a Provost's Travel to Library Collections grant from Oregon State University. Portions of "Secrecy and Disclosure in Fieldwork," from William B. Shaffir and Robert A. Stebbins (Eds.), *Experiencing Fieldwork* (Sage, 1991), are reproduced in chapters 5 and 6 by permission. Elements of chapter 4 are excerpted from "From Morality to Scientism: The Codification of Ethics in Sociology," in Larry T. Reynolds and Ted R. Vaughn (Eds.), *The Sociology of Sociology Revisited* (General Hall, in press).

SECRECY AND FIELDWORK

RICHARD G. MITCHELL, JR.
Oregon State University

1. INTRODUCTION

This is a book about secrecy and its consequences for the human sciences.
It is intended for qualitative researchers in anthropology, sociology, social
work, health care, communications, and marketing and others who must
come to grips with secrecy in their own professional practices and in the
lives of those they study. I begin with two assumptions: that (a) secrecy
is fundamentally social, an attribute of relationships constructed, negoti-
ated, and maintained by intentional social actors; and (b) all social action
entails secrecy. Simmel (1906) asserted the latter long ago: "All commerce of men [and women] with each other rests upon the condition that
each knows something more of the other than the latter voluntarily reveals
to him" (p. 455).

   Secrecy is a pervasive feature of contemporary social life. It is man-
dated by law, professional edict, organizational policy, gaming strategies,
norms of decorum, and other expectations. Nuclear submarines cruise
secret routes at secret depths while, on board, poker-playing sailors keep
secret their hold cards and actual emotions. Physicians nearly always keep
secret the HIV status of their patients and, sometimes, the incompetence
of their colleagues. Social workers are required to keep secret much of their
clients' biographical data in routine cases and are legally bound to reveal
clients' secrets (for example, suspected involvement in child abuse or
other felonious crimes) in exceptional instances. In prisons, the informal

1

2

but potent inmate code obliges inmates to keep each other's secrets from guards. In the work world, corporate executives may keep secret declining profits and impending staff cutbacks. They act in the reasoned hope that W. I. Thomas was right, that situations defined as real may become real in their consequences. By concealing negative news, worker confidence and investor optimism may continue, productivity increase, and real competitive advantages may be achieved. Reciprocally, subordinates may keep secrets from supervisors by inflating production figures and reports of task difficulty and by concealing major performance errors in order to magnify their own apparent utility and competence.

Americans are ambivalent about secrecy. On the one hand, they cherish durable beliefs in an open society, one in which individuals' ideas and information can and will be freely exchanged (Lowery, 1972). On the other, they are concerned with inadequate controls over organizations that collect, assemble, and distribute data pertaining to individuals. Americans are perturbed (and entertained) both by muckraking media revelations of the untoward intimacies of politicians, evangelists, and corporate kingpins and by crusading reformers clamoring for greater controls over information pertaining to private persons, such as credit ratings, mailing lists, and government data collections. For some there is too much secrecy in places of power. For others there is not enough protection for personal secrets, that is, not enough privacy.[1] During the early 1990s, this expressed concern for secrecy increasingly stood in contrast to widespread media exhibitionism. On such shows as "Oprah" and "Sally Jessy Raphael," individuals competed to reveal the detailed personal intimacies of their lives to millions of television viewers. An estimated audience of 21 million tuned in February 6, 1992, to hear Gennifer Flowers confess her alleged affair with then-Arkansas Governor Bill Clinton (Jones, 1992, p. A4).

Beyond the secrecy found in all social action, secrets are an integral part of social science research and are by no means limited to covert inquiry. The logic of certain inductive strategies of investigation requires secrecy. The results of routine competency testing, for example, are judged valid only when teachers keep test answers secret from students until after the exam. Other secrets are kept when, unknown to them, subjects are segmented into experimental and control groups, presented with placebos, given spurious accounts of the purpose of investigation, confronted with blind testing, and so forth.[2] Qualitative researchers also keep secrets, crafting persona consonant with the expectations of those they study in order to gain entrance and acceptance in nonpublic action. Some past works of this sort are well known. Goffman assumed the role of assistant to the athletic director in preparing Asylums (1961), and Gans, in researching the Urban Villagers (1962), told the residents of North End of Boston he was doing a "recent history" of the area, not a sociological analysis. Gusfield (1955) told Womens' Christian Temperance Union leaders he was a "disinterested investigator of American social movements," during his study of temperance advocacy (p. 29). Rosenhan and his research colleagues had themselves admitted as patients (with the same reporting symptoms) to a variety of psychiatric hospitals to study patient-staff interactions (Rosenhan, 1973; see also Thorne, 1980, p. 287).

Social scientists, too, have long been ambivalent about, and concerned with, secrecy. For nearly three quarters of a century, they have debated the empirical, moral, and epistemological effects of revelation and concealment in research and upon those researched. Certain features are reoccurring in these debates. Secrecy and disclosure are represented as polarized phenomena, antonymous and mutually exclusive. They are defined largely as problems of method, of what social scientists do, particularly in covert research and participant observation. They are treated as wholly volitional, as the results of willful choices by rational actors, intentional attributes of interaction to be imposed on, or withheld from, the social world, not discovered therein. And they are vested with supra-empirical, ethical significance.

These typifications are unsatisfactory in several respects. In narrowing attention to methodological practices, social scientists leave unexplored the place and meaning of secrecy in the everyday world they seek to understand. Uncritically depicting secrecy as a volitional cosmetic to communication reinforces the positivist notion that careful attention to methodological routines gives researchers the ability to discern and communicate unambiguous truth across sometimes unexplored boundaries of language, culture, and situational events. Combining the focus on method with the cosmetic myth relocates secrecy outside the social, beyond the intersubjective realm of symbolic interaction, either by reducing it to the manifest character flaws of (greedy, self-serving) individuals (Kelman, 1970, 1972; Warwick, 1974, 1975), or reifying it into (repressive, autonomous) institutional policy (Shils, 1956). The a priori linkage of secrecy and ethics gives rise to debates at cross-purposes: fact versus value, the naturalistic fallacy (Moore, 1903), and *Wertürteilsstreit* (the Value Dispute, as it was called at the turn of the century), arguments rooted in incomparable, although seldom acknowledged, pretheoretical paradigm assumptions.

4

This volume explores these and related problems of secrecy as a social phenomenon in several ways. Chapter 2 defines secrecy as a social construct, then outlines its forms and contexts. When secrecy is understood as a generic and constantly transforming feature of all social action, ethnographers' identities are not so much given roles to be played as they are emergent products of fieldwork itself, forthcoming as researchers and subjects explore each other's cognitive and affective revelations and concealments. Chapter 3 illustrates three of these modal research relationships. The consequences of research for persons studied is widely held as the core ethical conundrum of the social sciences. Much has been written, for example, about the ethics of sociology, how researchers ought to go about relating to the subjects of their work in a moral manner, and much of this debate has been over secrecy. Chapter 4 considers two competing views of the moral and professional merits of covert research and suggests the effects of formally managing and restraining such work. Chapter 5 examines the possibilities of independent social science in an age of institutional credentialing and corporate sponsorship. Independence, it is argued, entails greater risks and requires greater responsibilities. But it also is a prerequisite to forms of knowledge otherwise unobtainable. Chapter 6 looks at a common myth about secrecy and research, the myth of cosmetic identity, a misunderstanding, I argue, that poses the greatest risk to quality fieldwork. In conclusion, I suggest that as researchers our identities are never cosmetic, casual disguises to be put on like a party wig or false mustache but consequential experiences that encompass and define us at the same time we seek, through our craft, to encompass and define the worlds we study.

The discussions throughout are grounded in experiences gained from divergent fieldwork, including two studies undertaken by colleague Eleen Baumann and myself during the 1980s. The first research was a study of mountaineers, that is, people who climb mountains as an avocation. The second examined survivalism. Survivalists are those persons who anticipate various kinds of imminent cataclysms—economic collapse, race war, nuclear attack, and so forth—and take steps to ensure their own postdisaster welfare. The public images of these two groups are quite different. If climbers could be characterized, as one nonclimbing interviewee suggested, as "courageous, freedom-loving athletes," [3] then survivalists might be summed by a media-spawned moniker "bomb-shelter paranoids armed for Armageddon." Both studies provide useful illustrations of secrecy in practiced fieldwork.

Notes

1. In practice, both executive and judicial government actions foster secrecy. The U.S. Constitution does not specifically mention privacy, but in the 1965 Supreme Court decision in *Griswold vs. Connecticut* an individual's right to privacy from undue government interference was recognized. The decision overturned a Connecticut law forbidding the sale of contraceptives on the ground that the law interfered with the private lives of married persons. Later this interpretation served as the basis for the *Roe vs. Wade* decision, the court finding in that instance that laws forbidding abortion unduly intruded into the private lives of pregnant women. As matters of administrative policy, and on the grounds of protecting individual rights, government agencies sometimes refuse to disclose information that might be useful to consumers, such as arrest records involving physicians and lawyers. On grounds of protecting corporate privacy, government investigatory agencies seal files at the conclusions of civil suits involving damages caused by malfunctioning products (Jones, 1992, p. A4).

2. Two examples are well-known. Education researchers Rosenthal and Jacobson (1968) studied the effects of teachers' expectations on pupils' performance by keeping secret certain students' achievement levels while providing instructors with bogus and exaggerated records for those students. In Briddell et al.'s (1978) study of the effects of alcohol on sexual aggression, subjects received alcoholic and nonalcoholic cocktails, variously identified correctly and as their opposites.

3. See Mitchell (1983), appendix, for results of a U.S. nationwide poll of nonclimbers' attitudes toward mountaineers.

6

2. DEFINING SECRECY

Secrecy as Social Action

What is a secret? In the literature of the ancient times, between Abraham and Noah lived the Mesopotamian hero-king Gilgamesh, a man like no other,

> *To whom all things are known;*
> *the King who knew the countries of the world.*
> *He was wise, he saw mysteries and knew secret things.*
> *(Sanders, 1960, p. 61)* [1]

With his incomparable courage and singular knowledge of things secret, Gilgamesh ruled an empire, resisted the temptations of Ishtar, crossed the boundless seas, and slew the mighty Humbaba. Four thousand years later, for a few dollars, lesser powers accrue to more common individuals who buy from the mail-order catalogue *Victoria's Secrets* to improve their social allure. Although separated by four millennia and many orders of grandeur, the secrets of Gilgamesh and Victoria have common qualities. Both are kinds of social relationships, conceived, constructed, and maintained in symbolic interaction. And, like all social action, from epic Sumerian myth to mundane modern commerce, they are provisional, not absolute, context dependent, and expressive as well as instrumental.

Secrecy is never complete. It is axiomatic that human behavior obtains its form and meaning in and through symbolic communication with others, either directly or in imaginative rehearsal or review (Blumer, 1969, p. 2). Thus secrecy can only be partial, incomplete. The perfectly concealed act, the occasion beyond defining, naming, or symbolic representation of other sorts, is outside the realm of social behavior and therefore outside sociological concern. Neither the entirely discrete intrapsychic event that remains unarticulated even in imagination nor the hypothetical motions of wholly autonomous institutions of which actors have no perception are relevant here.

Secrecy is relative, not absolute. Secrecy is always embedded in and interpreted through cultural contexts, meanings, and practices. Attempts to define secrecy in absolute terms as the opposite of some hypothetical condition of pure, transparent actuality presupposes that social scientists (if not ordinary persons) possess a precise, complete, and context- and value-free discourse (see Hesse, 1980, p. vii; D. N. Levine, 1985, pp. 1-44). [2] Ethnomethodologists have pointed out the impossibility of such discourse.

They note that all utterances are indexical, all take for granted and imply more than their face value. To keep no secrets, to be totally honest, to totally disambiguate each component of symbolic communication, to define each word, to provide historical and contextual qualifiers for each statement, and to spell out all motivations for and implications of the content and assertions in any interaction is a near-infinite task. Such an "unloading" of nuances, details, and ancillaries would, in practical terms, be untoward and nearly endless.

When moralists and researchers claim to have acted in "total honesty," they are often speaking not of information exchanged but of affect, of the feelings they had for their subjects. For example, Ortiz (1992) recently claimed, with emphasis, to have acted with total honesty in his research among the wives of high-profile professional athletes. However, Ortiz's (1991) published and presented accounts both suggest that total honesty meant something to him other than comprehensive delivery of facts. Indeed, he reported the care he took to keep secrets, to conceal from his informants certain information he judged would be harmful or hurtful to them: knowledge of their spouses' infidelities, of inequities in players' contractual conditions, news of impending layoffs, transfers, demotions, and the like. Ortiz sought to act as a comprehensively sympathetic other, not as a totally factual one. Ortiz kept secrets and had strong feelings about doing so. So, too, do other researchers and members. Dealing with secrecy calls for more than rational action, it calls for what Hochschild (1983) dubs emotion work, the intentional display of affect that is self-induced and managed in accordance with others' expectations.

The Context and Forms of Secrecy

Secrecy in social action is clarified by locating it conceptually in the context of other unknowns (cf. Akerstrom, 1990, pp. 1-26; Bok, 1983/1989, pp. 5-28) and differentiating its strategic motives and tactical effects.

UNKNOWNS

Unknowns are relatively specific, defined, and bounded intellectual deprivations of three sorts:

Ignorance (absent knowledge). Ignorance is the absence of knowledge accessible via at-hand epistemologies, knowledge presumed to be available for discovery and explanation within existing theoretical frameworks.

Ignorance is dispelled by reallocating resources to appropriate knowledge-generating institutions, devices, and personnel, the products of which are presupposed to be new and valid truths.

Mysteries (inaccessible knowledge). Mysteries are phenomena perceived as arising independently of conventional modes of knowledge production and beyond the scope of accepted truth claims. Mysteries may be treated in two ways. In the first instance, their alienness is denied. They are classified and expressed in familiar terms, treated as no more than unlikely instances of known classes of events. Such is the case, for example, in rationalist anthropologists' interpretations of native magical practices as merely crude utilitarianism, as poor science (e.g., Horton, 1967/1979; Jarvie, 1960/1979; Jarvie & Agassi, 1970/1979; Winch, 1964/1979). Alternatively, mysteries may be accepted as irreducible to conventional discourse and encountered on their own terms. Understanding of mysteries in these contexts is only possible through a transcendence of the natural attitude, the everyday world of experience and perception. Although all scientific discourse is an attempt to reformulate the exotic in conventional terms, this reformulation may at times be intentionally tentative and incomplete. Authors may seek to retain an evocative, poetic quality in their accounts as in Castaneda's (1968) dialogues with Don Juan.

Secrets (denied knowledge). The principal topic of this volume, secrets, may be understood as knowledge that is available but unequally distributed. Approaching secrets involves access to privileged networks of information exchange.

SECRETS

Secrecy is one aspect of a broader process of impression management that may be referred to as concealment. Concealment is of two sorts, translocating phenomena out of sight and out of mind. Physical objects are concealed by being hidden, displaced from public and/or accessible locales. Information is kept secret by minimizing the range and content of certain communications. Survivalists, for example, hide their crisis time supplies in remote cabins, underground caches, or basement nooks and keep these locations secret from all but family members and other intimates.

Strategic secrets are divisible into altruistic, egoistic, and normative forms. The captured soldier's concern for his comrades may motivate altruistic secrecy, manifested in a stubborn refusal to reveal anything but name, rank, and serial number, even under duress. The hormone-driven undergraduate male may employ a stratagem of egoistic secrecy, of masking his lust and feigning love, in hopes that apparent moderation will win favors from his dates. The child who comments candidly on the body odor of an adult guest quickly learns that normative secrecy is expected, when mother admonishes, "We do not talk about things like that in this house!"[3]

Tactical secrets may be classified as ethnocentric, egocentric, or resource focused. Ethnocentric secrets are employed to protect information that, if revealed to outsiders, enemies, or other nonintimates, might be used to disparage or impugn group members collectively, reducing intergroup status. For example, some ardently racist survivalist organizations (not all survivalist groups are racist) seek to minimize their apparent prejudice in public pronouncements while continuing to foment interracial animosities among their members.[4] Egocentric secrets guard information regarding individuals' historical or constitutive attributes or behaviors that if known to other group members might result in loss of intragroup status. Novice climbers, for instance, soon learn to suppress any references to a personal work history in real estate development, logging, mining, or other vocations stigmatized by the environmental-activist majority of advanced climbers.[5] Resource-focused secrets are used to conceal information that if revealed to competitors might result in loss of privileged access to valued material assets. The location of a survivalist family's wilderness retreat or, for mountaineers, the coordinates of a major unclimbed peak are such secrets. Advertisers claim that secret ingredients and modes of manufacture lend distinction to cosmetics, investment schemes, study aids, food preparation utensils, beverages, items of attire, and other mundane commodities. They tout the advantages of "ancient secrets" or "secrets of the Orient" in helping (usually) rich, (sometimes) famous, and (occasionally) wise men, and (almost always) beautiful women, achieve their wealth, wit, craftiness, sex appeal, and popularity. In such contexts, secrecy is a resource for sale, an edge over competitors in impression management and other status negotiations.

Finally, those who employ secrecy either for strategic or tactical purposes do so with ambivalence. Survivalists, for example, are ambivalent about concealing their identities and inclinations. They realize that secrecy protects them from the ridicule of a disbelieving majority, but enforced separatism diminishes opportunities for recruitment and information

10

exchange. Survivalists also know what Simmel (1955) or, for that matter, what Shakespeare's Henry IV [6] might have told them, namely, that hypothesizing predatory enemies from whom information and resources must be protected serves to coalesce groups in collective purpose and elevates the apparent worth of existing knowledge and possessions.

In practice the security measures of all groups and individuals become a compromise effort of dual purposes: to deny the least sympathetic of other people access to information that might be used for invidious purposes and at the same time attempt to tailor their public images to what they perceive as nonmembers' sympathies. Thus no social behavior is absolutely secret, only relatively unknown.

Secretive survivalists eschew telephones, launder their mail through letter exchanges, use nicknames and aliases, and carefully conceal their addresses from strangers. Yet, often in my own research, once I was invited to group meetings, I found them cooperative respondents. Some volunteered outright to "tell their stories," as they called extended interviewing. Others, shy of one-on-one questioning, to my surprise, provided extensive written autobiographical and speculative essays. One group asked me to compose a group newsletter on my word processor. I agreed and almost immediately became the recipient of a steady stream of members' written opinions and perceptions. Being appointed editor of the newsletter, *The Survival Times*, in turn legitimated my use of tape recorders and cameras at group gatherings, provided me with an entree to survivalist groups elsewhere around the country, and underscored the wisdom of the pragmatic fieldworker's creed:

If the front door isn't open, try the back. If they don't like you as Tweedle Dum, then go as Tweedle Dee. (Anonymous)

Successful empirical sociology depends on understanding the ways social actors, including researchers of all sorts, manage secrecy and disclosure of their motives, identities, and practices.

Notes

1. Recommended is the English translation by Sanders (1960), titled *The Epic of Gilgamesh*. Cited material is from the first paragraph of the prologue to the first book of the epic, "Gilgamesh King of Uruk" (p. 61).
2. In common usage, secrecy is less than an antithesis to facticity than it is merely an obstruction to knowledge, a veil, distortion, or incomplete or inaccurate representation of the

obdurate world. It is presumed that antecedent to secrecy are more ontologically primary realities: valid but untold truths, actual but unreported facts, genuine but unshared intimacies, and other incontestable, concrete phenomena.

3. As a technique for social control, employers and parents often insist on the obverse of secrecy from subordinates. They proclaim the wisdom of the best-known portion of *Apohthegms*, by Richard Watley, the Archbishop of Dublin. "Honesty is the best policy," parents and employers insist. What goes unmentioned in this socialization lecture is that parents and superordinates may not hold themselves to the same standard. Nor do they often stress the rest of the Archbishop's aphorism:

> *Honesty is the best policy;*
> *but he who is governed by that maxim*
> *is not an honest man.*
> (Watley, 1953, p. 565)

4. At one national conference of survivalists, general assembly speakers repeatedly stressed the likelihood of imminent race-based civil war to the all-White membership while the leaders of smaller classes outlined specific preparations of this conflict. However, the conference program, made available to the curious press, offered only this equivocal reference to race.

> This particular Conference and Survival Seminar is for those of the White Race only. While the Christian-Patriots Defense League accepts membership and works with all races, it is always on a "Equal but Separate" basis. We are totally against integration and its subsequent destruction of races. Conferences and meetings for other races are held at other places.

5. Ponse (1967) provides other examples of both ethnocentric and egocentric secrets within lesbian subculture.

6. As Henry IV lay dying, he knew his son's succession to the throne would be challenged and his ability to rule beset with trouble (*The Second Part of Henry the Fourth*, Act IV, scene V). His advice?

> *Therefore my Harry,*
> *Be it thy course to busy giddy minds*
> *With foreign quarrels.*
> (ll. 212-214)

3. SECRECY AND THE RESEARCHER

To begin discussion of secrecy and the researcher I would like to stress two points recurrent throughout this text. First, the researcher's autonomy in fieldwork is realistically limited; second, her or his relationships with studied peoples are inseparably and simultaneously both cognitive and affective.

The Myth of Autonomy

The notion of the "researcher role" as an autonomous, self-directed creation should not be over-stressed. Fieldworkers do not claim, assume, or take their research roles with the vigor or assurance these active verbs might suggest. Qualitative investigators are well aware that the roles they play in the field are not strictly and exclusively of their own choosing. They may seek to present themselves in one manner or another, as a friend, disinterested bystander, or novice, but subjects can and usually do reinterpret, transform, or sometimes altogether reject these presentations in favor of their own. During his 2-year research sojourn to acutely segregated South Africa in the early 1960s, van den Berghe attempted to act, according to the dictates of his conscience, as if race was of no consequence. This behavior was accounted for in a variety of ways by the South Africans. He was viewed by Whites as a Communist agitator, an odd foreigner who had not yet learned to "handle the Natives" (van den Berghe, 1967, p. 189), or as merely socially inept. Blacks classified his behavior as that of a police informer, agent provocateur, missionary do-gooder, or paternalist (van den Berghe, 1967, p. 190). Virtually no one, White or Black, understood his actions as expressions of the nonmaterialistic, Gandhian socialism to which he was personally committed. The direction of influence and information flow between researchers and actors may likewise be fluid and problematic. Patrick (1973, p. 142) noted that during his work with Glasgow juvenile gang members it was sometimes difficult to discern who was conning or converting whom. Sutherland's (1975) research among the Rom gypsies was confounded by the routine gypsy practice of misrepresenting one's identity and intent as an accepted form of normal discourse (see also Bulmer, 1982, pp. 234-235). Peneff's (1985) experiences in Algeria, recounted in chapter 5, provide another example.

Qualitative research roles are, in practice, tentative offerings, possible forms of self, subject to negotiation and to the vicissitudes of the action

13

settings. The mistaken belief that the researcher's role is unmitigated by those whom he or she studies remains the positivist's unachievable hope. Indeed the distinction between research and other self-conscious action is precise and unequivocal only in retrospect.[1]

Reason and Feeling

The symbolic interactionist recognizes the inseparability of cognition and affect in all communication. No sustainable reasoned program is without valence or cathexis; no more-than-fleeting passion is without object and method.[2] Johnson (1977) made it clear that rational cognitive efforts— even in their most refined and formal incarnation, namely, scientific investigation—remain embedded in and shot through with passions and other potent feelings, such as compelling intrinsic curiosity, self-doubt, fear of failure, embarrassment, and befuddlement. Weber agreed. Whereas Weber's theory of bureaucracy, in particular, is often interpreted as a discourse on the omnipresence of rationality in modern life, Hilbert (1987) demonstrated that this interpretation is an unsubstantiated reading, of convenience to structuralists precommitted to that view. Weber reserved unexpressive rationality for the limiting case, what he called "objectively correct rationality" (cited in Brubaker, 1984, p. 53), the ideal typification of scientific method. The rational activity of daily affairs is entwined with actions that are fraught with considerable irrational expressivity. In Weber's view, persons choose to act in rational and calculating fashions predominately because they hold two sorts of subjective, nonrational feelings toward those processes. Individuals may pursue rational calculation and cognitive control, *wertrational* in Weber's terms, as an intrinsic good, a desirable and proper form of conduct in its own right. In the alternative of *zwecktrational* action, rationality is employed as utilitarian means of achieving what persons sense are valued and desirable ends. In both instances, rational behaviors are the expression of subjective feelings. Weber and Unamuno (cited in Douglas & Johnson, 1977, p. 15) reached similar conclusions. Much rationality arises from irrationality and serves irrational purposes, that is, impassioned, subjective, and cathected ones. The centrality of emotion in all social experience is elaborated elsewhere in this series of monographs by Kleinman and Copp (1993).

Ethnographic investigations seldom fail from a lack of data alone. More crucial are the distortions that occur when the cognitive and affective attributes of relationships with subjects grow out of balance, when perceptions

14

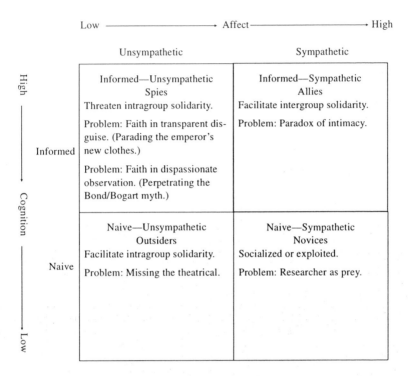

Figure 3.1. Cognition, Affect and Perception of the Researcher's Role

of shared mutual sympathies are not roughly commensurate with shared information. These problems may be highlighted by examining four hypothetical research roles (see Figure 3.1).[3] These roles are characterized as the combinations of two dimensions of researcher-subject relationships: the affective (sympathetic vs. unsympathetic) and the cognitive (naive vs. informed). Three of these research roles are elaborated below. The fourth, the notion of the researcher as spy, is considered separately in chapter 6.

Research Roles

THE NAIVE-SYMPATHETIC ROLE

Whatever fieldworkers intend their roles to be, they are most often perceived initially as naive sympathizers. Members may consider if, and how, persons new on the scene can be recruited to their cause, movement, or life-style. If researchers are perceived as potential recruits they may be given special treatment. They may be socialized, tested, indoctrinated, taught, and gradually granted positions of increasing intragroup responsibilities. This is an ideal position from which to learn of the subjects' meaning-world, but it is not the only way naive sympathizers can be treated. If members sometimes ask "Can this person be recruited?" they as often ponder "How can this individual be exploited?"

Problem: Researcher as prey. There is danger here for the ethnographer who assumes that information he or she receives is offered in good faith, that subjects are reciprocating his or her overtures in mutual trust and respect. The gratifying presence of a steady flow of responses to inquiries may lull investigators into the belief that their affective relationships with subjects are progressing apace, that they are gaining subjects' sympathies and acceptance. Subjects may view the relationship differently. They may see researchers as what M. L. Wax (1980) called prey (fair game, suckers, marks) whose pro-member sympathies and/or desire for information provide easy means by which they may be exploited for gifts, favors, or other advantages. Fieldworkers must remain aware that the apparent cooperativeness of subjects may be part of intentional self-serving efforts to warranty a continued supply of such goods and services as the researcher is able to provide. I was reminded of this possibility, even in mundane matters, during the 1991 Stone Symposium of the Society for the Study of Symbolic Interaction.

Being short of travel funds, Eleen Baumann and I had driven an on-loan, oversized farm truck/camper from Oregon to the meeting headquarters in downtown San Francisco. Arriving at night, amid city-center congestion, we were relieved to find a parking lot across from the conference hotel. Thankfully, a lot attendant materialized just as we turned into the crowded facility. The attendant volunteered information, explaining the regulations: Park anywhere, $5 for 12 hours of occupancy. When I asked about security, he offered reassurance that the lot was safe and walked about with me, pointing out the most illuminated and convenient spots. Then he provided assistance in directing the delicate backing operation required to fit our cumbersome rural vehicle into a compact urban space. And he collected the $5. We were pleased with this courteous and timely treatment until we left the lot and encountered the panhandlers on the corner. They put us straight. They pointed out the fee box at the lot's corner. Its instructions read, approximately, "Self-service parking. This lot maintained by the City of San Francisco. Select space. Deposit fee in corresponding slot. $2 for 12 hours." The "attendant," they told us, was an aging con man who worked the lot at night for out-of-town marks. I tipped the panhandler informants, put money in the fee box, and vowed to keep in mind that friendly, forthright hosts are not necessarily honest ones (see also R. H. Wax, 1971).

There is, of course, reciprocity in some exploitive relationships, which may be actively sought by researchers, both as a nominal compensation for subjects' assistance and as a token of good faith. During Ortiz's (1992) investigations of star athletes' spouses, he made himself useful variously by "babysitting, hanging curtains, running errands, house-hunting, house sitting, and helping to move in and unpack" (p. 13), as well as collecting articles on wives' husbands for their information and scrapbooks and writing articles for a wives' newsletter. In his study of Single Room Occupancy hotel patrons, Rollinson (1990) found that "helping out with messages, the delivery of mail, or other items was essential in gaining their trust" (p. 192). Fox (1987) reports that she was "able to gain the trust of some key members" among the punker subculture by "running errands for them, buying them drinks and food, and driving them to pick up their welfare checks and food stamps" (p. 347). Liebow (1967, pp. 243, 253) similarly provided transportation and shared money and favors with his informants.

The process of research itself may also hold utility for those researched. During his yearlong investigation of a California-based community mental health center, Brown (1989) came to be viewed by staff as an integral and useful part of the center's activities. Brown's professional credentials, access to incoming patients (even in advance of intake clinicians), and familiarity with clinic procedures were perceived as a valuable resource. He was consulted by staff on the course of their own research and future directions for clinic procedures and even provided input on specific ongoing cases (Brown, 1989, p. 186; see also Cassell, 1978, p. 138).

As previously noted, being put to use by survivalists as a newsletter editor, journalist, and photographer provided me with access to persons and information otherwise out of ready reach: so, too, did my service as a cold-weather survival instructor, computer programmer, and speech-writing consultant, among other capacities in which I was requested to assist various survivalist groups. None of these roles were solicited or self-appointed. All represented roles to which I was assigned by members in their attempts to make some use of me.

THE NAIVE-UNSYMPATHETIC ROLE

Naive-unsympathetic others provide members with contradistinctions that impel intragroup solidarity. These outsiders serve variously as the butt of jokes, objects of ridicule, and baselines for other invidious distinctions, against which members' outlooks and activities are affirmed as wise and appropriate. Survivalists justify their own rationales and preparations by comparing them to the "doomie apathy" and "doomie myths" [4] such as nonsurvivalists' belief in apocalyptic nuclear winter. Mountaineers set themselves apart from, and above, unathletic "flatlanders" and "armchair adventurers." This is not to suggest that outsiders are considered impotent. Members do not ignore the potential of outsider influence but may attempt to manipulate it by public self-presentations that are intentionally dramatized exaggerations of members' positions, practices, and prowess.

Problem: Missing the theatrical. The danger to fieldworkers here lies in missing the theatrical aspect of these communications, in taking them at face value as unadorned expressions of subjects' worldviews. Media accounts of survivalist activities have been particularly prone to this kind of distortion, often reporting apocryphal tales and intentionally extreme statements of ideology and program as everyday survivalist events and views. When these secondhand reports serve as the principal bases of analyses, such as Coates's (1987) sensationalizing of survivalism in *Armed and Dangerous* or, to a lesser extent, Ullman's (1964) romanticized *The Age of Mountaineering*, the error is compounded. Uncritical readings of survivalist periodicals are a fertile source of such misunderstandings.

Survivalist periodicals. In some accounts, the phenomenon of survivalism is represented essentially as a technical process, a matter of acquiring appropriate implements and supplies and guarding these against the predations of others. In these arguments, interest in and ownership of specialized material resources, particularly weapons and other combat equipment, are the principal features defining survivalist membership and commitment (Linder, 1982; Meyers, 1982; Peterson, 1984). This view of survivalists as combat-equipped, would-be warriors derives in part from and is substantiated by the content of commercial publications claiming to serve the survivalist market. Since the early 1980s, magazines like *American Survival Guide* (ASG), *S.W.A.T. —Survival Weapons and Tactics*, and *Guns and Action* (formerly *Survive*) have sold 70,000 to 90,000 monthly copies touting tool-mediated solutions to survival problems. In product critiques, sometimes barely distinguishable from ads, readers learn that Ultra Shock bullets produce "greater wound cavities with more penetration" (ASG, 1984c, p. 43), Nighthawk carbine offers "firepower, fast and furious in 9mm Parabellum" (ASG, 1984b, p. 8), and the "Foxfire high-tech crossbow reflects silent lethality" (ASG, 1984a, p. 74). There are articles on custom survival knives costing up to $250, umbrella and cane swords, and other cutting-edged weapons disguised as lipsticks, fountain pens, belt buckles, and credit card holders. There are bullet-"proof" vests, caps, umbrellas ($1,200 for the 48-in. size), and clipboards. To these add camouflaged shirts, pants, jackets, caps, handkerchiefs, pens, lighters (two-pack, $4.95), hiking shorts, boots, shoe laces, suspenders, and underwear. Also offered to the would-be survivalist are GI-style dog tags, blow guns, night-vision gunsight systems, armored personnel carriers, and books on *Secrets of the Ninja, How to Avoid Electronic Eavesdropping, How to Find a Girl to Love You,* and *Torture, Interrogation and Execution.*

This martial gadgetry is less, and more, than it seems. It is less than an unobtrusive measure of survivalist possessions and needs. Survivalists of my acquaintance read these magazines only sporadically and then with bemused and often incredulous fascination. It was the technological elegance and sophistication of the products, rather than their utility in defense, that was the principal attraction for my survivalist informants. To hear such equipment discussed in typical post-potluck-meeting conversations would remind the listener of other male technical banter. Gun talk, as I labeled this form of conversation in my early fieldnotes, is much like car talk, a blend of guess-what-you-can-buy-now enthusiasms and recitations of performance statistics, with reoccurring emphasis on power and speed. The objects discussed could as well be high-lift cam shafts, turbochargers, or high-performance ignition and exhaust systems. Neat stuff to discuss and a great way to show one's knowledge of manly and important things, but not very practical to own. And survivalists like to think of themselves as eminently practical. Nor should interest in these provocative implements be taken as evidence of survivalist predelictions to violent action.

For survivalists, this equipage has special meanings. For them, guns, knives, camouflage clothing, and the like are not the essential implements of a practiced trade but symbols by which they dramatize their personal competence. Many survivalists feel estranged by theoretical, abstract, and collective solutions to survival problems, but they are reassured by possession of what they perceive as potent technology and fascinated by technical detail and the operation of standardized mechanisms. To survivalists, tools are more emblematic than utilitarian; they are more signs of rational preparation and commitment than mortal and obdurate necessities. Survivalists measure readiness in terms of the accumulation and display of "practical" equipment and supplies and the verbal substantiation of claimed skills, not in demonstrated acts of violence.

The Cascade Mountain Volunteers are typical of one survivalist type. Core members share barbecues, lawn mowers, and fence lines on a suburban cul-de-sac. All seven members have other things in common: camouflage uniforms, distinctive shoulder patches, .45-caliber semiautomatic pistols, military assault rifles, a 28-page manual of operating procedures, and an authoritarian hierarchy from commander to infantryman. They also share CB radio frequencies, monthly outings, target practice, inspections, and a detailed emergency-time escape plan that includes attacks on a rural police station, robbery of a food storage facility, and capture of a major highway bridge. Yet the Volunteers are much less fearsome than these accoutrements and plans make them seem. Their firearms are state-of-the-art, their ammunition dry and plentiful, their garb and demeanor impressively military, but they are far from ready soldiers. Attendance at the mandatory monthly meetings in which I participated averaged 60%. The commander's orders elicited discussion and debate as frequently as obedience. Members were no longer young or slim or well-conditioned. Their backpacks traveled mostly by pickup truck. Only two members could read a map or compass. Only one member knew CPR. Their authentic Vietnam-style jungle combat clothing was nostalgic and looked snappy at meetings but was ill-suited to the cold, damp outdoors of their native Pacific Northwest. When it rained, these survivalists, like many others, usually stayed home and cleaned their unused guns, counted their ammunition, played show-and-tell with other group members, thumbed through survivalist magazines, and talked about the daggers and bullet proof umbrellas and armored personnel carriers they did not own.

THE INFORMED-SYMPATHETIC ROLE

Informed-sympathetic others are seen as allies with whom members characteristically affirm intergroup solidarity. In the metaphor of theater, allies are backstage visitors, free to examine the make-up and props, with whom members commiserate, rejoice, and confirm the worthiness of their craft. Allies do keep secrets, as do members one from another, but in these relationships secrecy is often maintained by mutual consent, reflecting a common notion of proprietary boundaries between the public and the private.

There are two dangers here for those researchers who achieve the status of presumably sympathetic and allied insiders more rapidly than they acquire members' knowledge. This imbalance may, in the case of such pseudo-membership, give rise to actions suggesting personal or professional incompetence, or to the paradox of intimacy, in which affective ties constrain the acquisition of knowledge available to nonintimates.

Problem: Personal incompetence. Some researchers may appear more knowledgeable than they are. Front-work facades—costuming, general appearances, and the like—may give the impression that investigators possess insider knowledge and sympathies when little or none exists. Hamabata (1986) describes the beginnings of his dissertation research among the elite business-owning families of Japan as a painful time of misattribution. His "first (miserable) six months in Tokyo" were a time he "was without life, a specter of sorts, a ghost [who] . . . only became a person with accompanying identity, with roles and obligations by . . . blundering about, by blundering across boundaries of culture, class and sexuality" (p. 354). As a third-generation American of Japanese ancestry, Hamabata encountered recurrent misunderstandings at the outset of his fieldwork. Being phenotypically Japanese and having introductory connections to Japanese society through wealthy industrial families, he was often mistyped as an insider, someone socially connected and culturally knowledgeable. These appearances were incorrect. His American upbringing and 3 years of language training left him poorly prepared for the subtleties of Japanese social life. He found himself repeatedly embarrassing hosts and befuddling others with his inabilities. He reports being unable to give lucid directions to a cab driver or seat himself properly at a buffet dinner (without usurping the guest of honor's place). Elsewhere he could not manage to avoid appearing as a sexual predator at mixed-sex social occasions or even walk with decorum through a pillow strewn room.

Hamabata (1986) resolved this disparity between apparent and actual cultural knowledge by intentionally emphasizing his artlessness and immaturity. He began referring to himself in familiar and diminutive linguistic forms, forms usually reserved for children, and encouraged others to address him in similar fashion. He repeatedly emphasized his student status, a status strongly associated with youthfulness and naivete in elite Japanese society. When improprieties occurred, Hamabata began managing the resultant embarrassment by outbursts of audacious childlike behavior. Over time, these combined efforts provided him with a workable identity, one less competent and knowledgeable than appearances suggested, what Hamabata (1986) called an "incomplete Japanese" (p. 356).

Problem: The paradox of intimacy. Genuine intimacy carries with it implicit expectations constraining the scope and forms of inquiry. Trusted insiders are expected to understand and assiduously avoid displaying certain kinds of inquisitiveness. A breach of these expectations is particularly dishonoring when committed by intimates, although novices may be permitted an occasional faux pas. Thus the paradox of intimacy. A high degree of trust achieved early in an investigation may actually curtail researchers' freedom to look and ask (e.g., Molstad, 1991). Researchers may feel obligated to reciprocate affective intimacy by uncritically honoring hosts' inhibitions toward certain forms and topics of study. The course of investigations may be redirected away from proscribed but significant phenomena, or relevant data may be omitted from written and other reports.[5]

Having achieved relatively rapid acceptance among advanced mountaineers at the beginning of my fieldwork obviated certain important lines of investigation. Although mountaineering elites cordially encouraged technical questions about how climbing was accomplished, inquiries regarding climbers' affect and motive were strongly discouraged. Any variant of "Why do people climb?" or similar questions regarding the feelings and emotions climbers might have on the mountain or about mountaineering were treated as distinctly untoward. I learned that expressivity was a private matter among climbers, a topic about which genuinely knowledgeable mountaineers would not and should not inquire. When *Mountain Experience* (Mitchell, 1983) was subsequently published it received vituperative criticism from elements of the climbing community, specifically for its discussion of climber motive and affect. One reviewer called me a "pretender," another called me a "spy." Before considering the validity of these accusations and what it means to be a "spy," it is important to examine the debate among social scientists themselves concerning secrecy in research.

Notes

1. As Lofland and Lofland (1984) noted, qualitative research often begins when researchers intensify the interest, curiosity, and reflection they devote to everyday experience. Fox's (1987, p. 346) study of punk subculture grew out of her own participation in the punk bar scene and was aided by her personal preference for punk hairstyle and fashion. Similarly, Katovich and Reese (1987) analyzed the identities and membership processes of patrons in an urban bar that they patronized themselves over a period of several years. Basirico's (1986) investigations of stained-glass artisans and entrepreneurs was based on his experience as the part owner and full-time operator of a stained-glass business for 7 years. Richards (1986, p. 324) first discovered the management strategies of nursing home personnel not as a researcher but as a (frustrated and angry) son seeking to ensure quality treatment for his Alzheimer's-stricken mother.

2. To Weber's (1968) ideal typification of a special affect-free scientific rationality should be added the fictive heroines and heroes of pulp literature and popular films. Caught up in affect-dominated lives, these caricatures are perpetually consumed by omnipresent "love" in romance novels or driven by insatiable "rage" over some dishonor in Westerns and other male action movies. Although such figures may be reoccurant in popular culture and adolescent fantasy, empirical instances are rare.

3. Discussions of fieldwork roles have an extensive history, most recently and definitively elaborated by Adler and Adler (1987) in *Membership Roles in Field Research*. Alternatively, Bulmer (1982, pp. 232-241), in his critique of covert research, developed a catalogue of research roles based on degrees of revelation and concealment. Also see Gold (1958). The typology of roles proposed here is not intended as an alternative to the schemes others have previously provided but merely serves as a means of highlighting the range and forms of secrecy's effects.

4. The premier issue of the first commercial survivalist magazine, *Survive*, published in the fall of 1981, featured as its lead article survivalist entrepreneur Bruce Clayton's "Nuclear Nonsense: Dispelling 'Doomie' Myths" (Clayton, 1981). Clayton's "doomie" expressions caught on and are still in use among survivalists.

5. This general process of self-censorship in fieldwork was the topic of papers presented at the 1989 American Sociological Association's annual meetings in the section on qualitative methodology (see especially Adler & Adler, 1989).

23

4. THE DEBATE OVER SECRECY

To assert that secrecy is omnipresent in social action is not to imply that fieldworkers are disinterested in its consequences. To note that the identities we present in the field are subject to members' interpretations does not mean that we are unconcerned with the roles we play or the impressions we make. Nor is the issue of secrecy in research without controversy. Social scientists, no less than lay persons, are profoundly animated and divided by the secrecy issue and fervent in championing various positions pro and con. Qualitative fieldwork is often identified as the locus of covert research and is therefore central to these debates. Fieldworkers, in turn, are often called on to justify what research secrets are appropriate for themselves, their subjects and their professions. This chapter examines arguments for and against covert research with the aim of helping fieldworkers make those judgments and justifications. Examples from sociology are used throughout.

In 1989, the American Sociological Association (ASA) completed the most recent revision of its Code of Professional Ethics governing the practice of sociology by association members. This is the latest formal statement of the discipline's ethical orientations, from a contentious dialogue begun in 1951, pursued with vigor through various committees and drafts over much of the next two decades (Dorn & Long, 1974, p. 32; Rhoades, 1981; Schuler, 1969), and continued to the present (Love, 1989; Mitchell, 1990; Walters, 1989). In the course of this debate, two sorts of claims have been made regarding sociologists' ethical responsibilities in conducting research and the appropriateness of covert investigation strategies. These I will refer to as the liberal and humanist positions. Both liberals and humanists concur that the social sciences are indeed consequential and, without redirection, are also potentially injurious. However, they disagree as to the locus and scope of the hazards posed by unfettered research, particularly covert investigations, and the effects of codes in curtailing abuse. In general, liberals are opposed to covert research and concern themselves with the deportment of individuals engaged in the production of knowledge. The distribution of knowledge and knowledge production resources, and the utility of covert research, receives humanists' principal attention.

Liberal Opposition to Covert Research

Liberals include Erickson (1967), Bulmer (1982, pp. 3-12, 217-251), Kelman (1965, 1968, 1967/1970, 1972), and Warwick (1974, 1975). In a neopositivist spirit, these critics find principal fault with the misuse of science in what they deem flawed research procedures. Their ethical criticisms have sought to improve and refine mainstream sociology by championing prohibitions against "deception" (Kelman), "misrepresenting" (Erickson), "lying," and other "secretive," nontransparent methods of investigation, methods liberals judge intrinsically harmful to subjects (or inconvenient to their own research).[1] Liberal advocates proclaim a teleological commitment to truth in all things (Bulmer, 1982, pp. 3-12, 217-251). They represent formal ethics codes as necessities, as systemic defense mechanisms against what Abbott (1983) dubbed "the inherent social danger of uncontrolled expertise" (p. 864). As these arguments go, professional competence and capacity have expanded in many areas with the growth of scientific progress, technological development, and rational organization, giving rise to increased need for regulation of those who command this new efficacy, including social scientists.

Liberal arguments have come to represent the official view of ASA as well as that of other disciplines' organizations and have been formalized in codes of professional ethics. In various forms, these codes operationalize ethical deportment in terms of adherence to legalistic prescriptions and proscriptions, the sine qua non of which has become the procedurally proper acquisition of informed consent. Studied peoples are conceptualized as rational actors principally needing "facts" to determine and act in their own best interests, and consent practices are presumed to provide adequate bases for these judgments.[2]

Although informed consent requirements pose little more than a technical inconvenience for mainstream social science, they represent a significant inhibition to qualitative fieldwork. Consider some particulars of the 1989 version of the ASA code in light of fieldworkers' experiences. That document requires researchers to assume foreknowledge of, and control over, the phenomena to be studied. They must be competent to foresee the results of their investigations to the extent that they can, with precision, differentiate "moderate risk" outcomes from "serious risk" ones, and these outcomes can be compared to the baseline "risks of everyday life."[3] Given these estimates, researchers must then construct "culturally appropriate" means of obtaining informed consent, sometimes tautologically prior to accessing the very cultures they may be seeking to understand (ASA, 1989, p. 3). Embedded in ASA's code [4] are further regulations, ones that forbid research in which "subjects can be identified" individually and where there is "risk of criminal or civil liability" or potential damage to "financial standing or employability" and research that involves "sensitive subjects," such as "illegal conduct, drug use, sexual behavior or use of alcohol" (American Association of University Professors, 1981, pp. 360, 366).

Interpretive researchers have raised objection to these regulations, particularly criticizing informed consent requisites on technical grounds. M. L. Wax (1977, 1980), Cassell (1978, 1980), Olesen (1979), and Thorne (1980) all contended that routinized consent is inapplicable to an everyday social world where interpersonal confidence is emergent and continually renegotiated. Others noted that complex consent forms and procedures may actually obscure rather than reveal researchers' intents (Applebaum, 1984, p. 33; Cassileth, Zupkis, Sutton-Smith, & March, 1980; Epstein & Lasagna, 1969; Roth et al., 1982).[5] Bond (1978), in considering the legal status of promised confidentiality, pointed out that for some subjects signing informed consent forms may even pose a potential liability when those forms are unprotected from subpoena and can be used to link individuals to illegal or otherwise stigmatizing activities.[6]

LIBERAL EVIDENCE

Although the liberal account has come to dominate the secrecy-ethics debate in the ASA and elsewhere, supporting evidence for the position is not abundant. In sociology, if not all the social sciences, convincing demonstrations of misused secrecy are hard to find. Neither the 1989 ASA code nor its predecessors offer data of any sort demonstrating the form or scope of ethical research transgressions by sociologists of the sort the code ostensibly inhibits. They contain no examples, no case studies, not even hypothetical instances. Instead of data, these codes provide hints and innuendoes that the situation is serious, warnings about "the potential for harm" (ASA 1989, p. 1), and suggestions of the risk that may arise in unspecified research circumstances. Elsewhere, evidence is also sparse.

In 31 years of published debate over secrecy in sociological research, from 1953 through 1984, 25 authors contributed material to 18 articles and commentary, comprising 89 pages of text in the *American Sociological Review* and the *American Sociologist*. In this extended discussion, only three cases of sociological research were cited as problematic, with liberal critics showing a tight centripetal dependence on two illustrative dark stars, *Project Camelot* (see Horowitz, 1965, 1967) and Humphreys's *Tearoom Trade* (1970). A Department of Housing and Urban Development-sponsored study of racial discrimination by real estate agents in cases where Black and White couples sought to rent advertised properties, cited once, provided the third illustration.

My own attempts to locate evidence of research impropriety, using ASA's archived records in the Library of Congress, were largely unproductive.[7] Records from the early 1960s chronicle repeated intensive efforts by the newly formed Committee on Professional Ethics to solicit case descriptions of ethical improprieties from ASA membership and other interested parties. These efforts produced fewer than two dozen recorded responses over a 3-year period. The responses received included several each of complaints regarding promotion and tenure procedures, graduate student rights and responsibilities, and a variety of issues of inter- and intracampus politics. However, only two cases dealt with research, and these two were the only instances found in the entire collection (an estimated 57,900 indexed items occupying 75 linear feet of shelf space). Reverend Blondino from the College of Our Lady of the Ozarks complained of "social engineering" by interviewers in Puerto Rico who volunteered birth control information to subjects, thus, in his judgment, "doing violence to the values of a social system in equilibrium" (G. Blondino, letter to the ASA Committee on Professional Ethics, December 8, 1961). A London-based sociology graduate student conducting participant observation among members of a religious sect was faulted for "never quite making clear the real and sole purpose of his research (academic), but letting the sect define him as someone interested in the sect itself even to the point of possibly joining" (F. Fontaine, letter to the ASA Committee on Professional Ethics, 1961). Considering this paucity of evidence for misused secrecy, how has the liberal argument against covert research been supported?

LIBERAL RHETORIC

Key to the success of liberal arguments is a rhetorical stratagem that equates secretive research methods with harmful research results. In the language of social constructionism, liberal arguments may be understood as the rhetorical practices of claims makers, advocates seeking the redefinition of some special-interest phenomenon as a social problem. Best (1987, 1990; Best & Horiuchi, 1985), in his skillful expansion of the works of Gusfield (1966, 1981) and Spector and Kitsuse (1977), point out two elements of constructed claims. First, these claims depend on dramatizable data of a special sort, what Best (1990) calls the "atrocity tale" (pp. 132-137), an intrinsically compelling case study of the problematic conditions being claimed. Second, they require "warrants" (see Toulmin, 1958; Toulmin, Rieke, & Janik, 1979, pp. 43-56), convincing, if not logical, arguments used to link these personified horror stories and their aggregates to the policies, programs, and other solutions claims makers propose.

In liberal claims making, atrocities are imported from medical research, then linked to the social sciences, most commonly through Stanley Milgram's obedience studies. The American Association of University Professors (AAUP) report, "Regulations Governing Research on Human Subjects: Academic Freedom and the Institutional Review Board," is now a wholly incorporated subset of the 1989 ASA Code of Professional Ethics and provides an example of this claims-making process (Schier, 1985).

The AAUP report begins with graphic description of a genuine atrocity tale, the Tuskegee study, a nearly 40-year project in which the U.S. Public Health Service tracked the syphilitic deterioration of 399 poor Black males who were misled by researchers into believing their ailments were being treated rather than merely observed (AAUP, 1981, p. 358). Next the report shifts attention to the "public anger" (AAUP, 1981, p. 358) aroused when the study became known and emphasizes that Tuskegee was not an isolated instance, "was not the only experiment on human subjects to anger the public" (AAUP, 1981, p. 358). The other instance the AAUP document cites is Milgram's investigation of obedience. Thus public anger, not demonstrable harm to subjects, becomes the report's common denominator between medical research and social science; and there is a common cause for this anger, namely, secrecy. According to the AAUP argument, public anger arose in both cases because researchers kept secrets, because both investigations "involved deception, indeed deception of such a kind as to cause considerable psychological discomfort to people who learn it was practiced upon them" (AAUP, 1981, p. 359). Therefore, the report concludes, "it is not merely medical research that needs regulating: social science research needs it too" (AAUP, 1981, pp. 358-359). In representing Milgram's work as typical of the hazards posed by social science and lumping his laboratory research together with the

28

Tuskegee investigations, the liberal warrant universalizes the need for restrictions against secrecy to sociology and elsewhere.

The liberal claim that nontransparent research in sociology should be forbidden can be unsympathetically restated this way: The Tuskegee investigators kept secrets, deceived subjects, and caused them to die (which angered the public). Milgram kept secrets and deceived subjects, causing them psychological discomfort (which angered the public). Sociology is essentially similar to these other sciences and therefore needs controls on its dangerous potential that forbid nontransparent research (in order to keep from angering the public). Apel (1982), Sjoberg (1983, p. 276), Djilas (1957), Konrad and Szelenyi (1979), and Abbott (1983) all proposed in various ways that liberals have a specific public in mind when they object to research secrecy, a public it is important not to anger for economic rather than moral reasons, namely, funding agencies.[8]

Sociologists are undoubtedly not blameless. Considering the volume and diversity of sociological research, some work is certain to have caused subjects embarrassment, concern, or worse. But these actions are not a salient part of the record on which liberal claims are made.[9] What does comprise a significant portion of the unpublished case materials and committee reports found in the ASA archives and elsewhere are not accounts of research-subject abuse but accounts that reflect a concern central to the humanist critique, the problem of external control over sociological enterprise, the problem of sponsorship.[10]

Humanist Advocacy for Covert Research

At the foundation of the humanist tradition are the concerns of C. Wright Mills, Alfred McClung Lee, Gideon Sjoberg, Lewis Coser, Arthur Vidich, and more recently Howard Becker, Peter Berger, and Jack Douglas. For these and other humanists the ethical problem in sociology lies deeper than the misuse of method. These humanists decry what they see as a fundamental misappropriation of part or all of the social science enterprise into the hands of a sometimes self-serving, privileged elite. Of primary concern to humanists is the potential of funding agencies, corporate gate-keepers, and intraprofessional moral entrepreneurs to curtail, redirect, co-opt, or delegitimate certain social science research. Humanists reproach informed consent routines specifically for their political regressiveness, for their utility in providing gatekeepers and elites with justifications to deny researchers access to the social settings they control (Douglas, 1976;

Galliher, 1973, 1980; Wilkins, 1979). Roth (1969) put it bluntly: "Insofar as codes of ethics make a claim to protecting the public against improper professional or business practices, the codes are a fraud. The way in which they are actually used tends to protect the fraternity against the public rather than the other way around" (p. 159). Anatole France observed that the law, in all its neutral majesty, prevents both the rich and poor alike from sleeping under bridges at night. We are reminded by Duster, Matza, and Wellman (1979) that codes serve similarly to protect the powerful and the weak from being studied without their explicit permission. There are radical, or "strong," and nominal, or "weak," readings of this position.

NOMINAL HUMANISM

The nominal or weak humanist reading represents secrecy as a symptom and instrument of interclass conflict. At mid-century, Fichter and Kolb (1953) stressed the sociologists' "practical as well as moral [obligations] to the source[s] from which resource funds are obtained" (p. 545) and to such other interested parties as factory managers, labor union officers, ministers, city officials, and others who might wish to make use of research results. However, by 1968, the proclaimed obligation of sociologists shifted from sponsors and interested others to studied peoples. This variant of humanism was clearly articulated by members of the student New Left movement of the 1960s, who argued that sociological research had become but a thinly veiled form of sophisticated surveillance over subjugated populations. Although some sociologists claimed their research to be dispassionate science, humanists warned that in fact it facilitated megacorporate interests in maintaining existing status differentials, controlling the domestic poor, and furthering imperialistic exploitation of the powerless abroad. Nicolaus's (1969) address to the ASA council in 1968 sharply dissented from the liberal outlook, charging that "the eyes of sociologists . . . have been turned downwards, and their palms upward," while they "stand guard in the garrison and report to the masters on the movements of the occupied populace" (p. 155; also see Nader, 1969; Rock, 1979). Ethnographers, too, were vilified as "the more adventurous" individuals who "don the disguise of the people and go out to mix with the peasants in the 'field,' returning with books and articles that break the protective secrecy in which a subjugated population wraps itself and make it more accessible to manipulation and control" (Nicolaus, 1969, p. 155). The ASA was not insensitive to this view. The council's proposed (but not adopted) Preamble to the first Code of Ethics cautioned against the misapplication of sociological knowledge. The council warned that "the results of sociological investigation may be of significant use to individuals in power . . . [and] creates the potential for political manipulation" (ASA, 1968, p. 318).

The New Left did not explicitly complain of the violation of ethics, a term they would probably dismiss as bourgeois rhetoric, but their implicit moral message was clear. Sociology, in the wrong hands, did harm to those upon whom its potency was directed (Warwick, 1980, p. 35). Also implicit in the weak humanist reading is the belief that secrecy is an appropriate stratagem for disadvantaged groups seeking buffers to scrutiny from above.

RADICAL HUMANISM

The radical or strong humanist position derives more from Hobbes than Marx. Emphasis shifts from the distribution of sociological knowledge to the means by which it is obtained. Radical humanists reject all forms of liberal-positivist and nominal humanist depictions of social life as cooperative and nonsecretive. In the strong reading, secrecy is accepted as a normal and expected attribute of human affairs within as well as between social strata. The phenomenal social world is presumed to be shot through with misinformation, evasion, lies, and fronts at every level, and research in kind—secret, covert, concealed, and disguised—is necessary and appropriate (Douglas, 1976, pp. 55-82).[11] Secrecy on the part of researchers is accepted, even urged, in implied utilitarian terms, as a necessary requisite to obtaining valued knowledge from reluctant and privileged sources (Dorn & Long, 1974; Douglas, Rasmussen, & Flanagan, 1977; Galliher, 1973, 1980).

The strong reading of the humanist position asserts what liberalism denies and nominal humanism ignores, that is, the implicit paradigm assumptions behind objections to secrecy. Those whose epistemologies depend on the assumptions of objective observers and observable objects perforce favor the notion of an orderly, consensual society of cooperative citizens, free and open in their exchanges of information. The researcher's job is understood to be the unidirectional transfer of information from the private to the public, from the concealed to the revealed. The investigator's task is to discover that which is hidden or kept secret by subjects (or that which remains unknown to them) and to hold these discovered truths to the light of scientific scrutiny. Fundamental to this method is the notion that all scientific hypotheses must be falsifiable through some crucial test. It is axiomatic to this view that subjects keep no relevant secrets; all that matters of their behavior and attitudes must be known, discovered, or controlled in the process of inquiry. Without this assumption, the crucial test, and with it the underlying epistemology, is either flawed or impossible. Secrecy has no permanent place in this form of scientific enterprise. Secrecy is something to be overcome in subjects and eschewed by researchers. Seldom are these paradigm assumptions mentioned outright in the debate over secrecy. Instead, objections are couched in moral terms and formalized in professional codes of ethics, but the implications remain clear.

Informed consent, for example, can be rationalized into quasi-contractual paper-signing rituals only when fundamental assumptions are made about the nature of social interaction, only when events and meanings, relationships, and collectivities are assumed to remain essentially unchangeable throughout the critical period of data collection (Cassell, 1978). Action settings must be imagined or manufactured that are closed for the duration of study. To avoid contravening code restrictions such as those imported from the AAUP (1981, p. 366), research must take place only where new, uninformed, or unconsenting persons are prohibited from coming into the research scene unbidden or unannounced, only where frontstage and backstage remain distinct, where no lovers fondle or quarrel; no strangers pick a fight; no one of his or her own accord drinks too much, smokes a joint, talks about his or her sex life, or otherwise engages in research-discrediting behaviors (see Thorne, 1980).

Professional ethics codes are traditionally discussed as if they narrowly proscribe organizational members' behavior only. In this limited sense, sociology's code, for example, expresses how sociologists themselves ought to act. But the radical humanist view suggests that the effects of the secrecy-ethics debate is more inclusive. When statements of how social scientists should conduct their researches carry with them taken-for-granted views of the social life to be studied, these statements are of enormous consequence. Directives for how social scientists should go about knowing the world influence what, for purposes of moral science, there is to be known. Thus, in the guise of prophylactic codes, positivism reasserts itself not merely as a utilitarian mode of discovery but as a procedural prerequisite to moral scientific enterprise. What positivism lost of its logical potency to philosophy of science critics in the 1950s was regained in the 1970s by defining, and claiming as its own, an exclusive path to the moral high ground. In the social worlds to which formal codes apply, qualitative fieldwork, particularly covert participant observation, is no longer merely intellectually irksome. It is ethically deficient. In that codified universe, moral science requires positivist methods.

As noted above, the liberal view has predominated in formal ethics of sociology, whereas humanist perspectives have largely been ignored. Perhaps this is not surprising. The humanist critiques are fundamentally disruptive to the status quo. They challenge the very legitimacy of sociology as a discipline—its internal order, system of rewards and strategic direction, even its basic epistemology. In the nominal humanist perspective, victimization is not limited to a few isolated research subjects but becomes the general fate of an entire disenfranchised social class. And most objectionable, the nominal humanist critique demotes the social science researcher from the villainous but potent role of callus machinator to that of funding agency toady or establishment dupe (Nicolaus, 1969, p. 155). Radical humanism goes further, undermining the fundamental sociological project of linking behavioral appearances with hypothetical social structures. By reassuring contrast, liberal ire has not been directed at the research practices of sociology's mainstream but at those on the margin and beyond, the laboratory psychologist, and the relatively low-status participant observer. As such, liberal complaints have posed little threat either to the vested interests of most sociologists or to powerful corporate entities and have offered a sort of breastplate of righteousness for those whose research agendas and practices avoided areas of identified controversy. In the liberal scheme, (a few) sociologists, not sociology, need to be held accountable. Collective-corporate ethical responsibility of the sort urged by nominal humanists is supplanted by particularistic attention to the ostensible misdeeds of individual researchers. Abbott (1983) reported similar adaptations in numerous other codes, all of which served to shift responsibility from the profession to the professional. That paradigm assumptions might influence these ethical judgments is not considered at all in the liberal account. In sum, although liberal-inspired codes have come to pose complex logistical challenges (or unsurmountable barriers) for those fieldworkers attempting to meet their requisites, they still offer little guidance for those seeking to deal responsibly with secrecy in the obdurate social world. Chapter 5 considers the issue of responsible secrecy in the special case of independent fieldwork.

33

Notes

1. Bonacich (1970) objected to nontransparent methodology in utilitarian terms. He argued that the "problem of deception in social psychological experiments" can be defended as "rational" for individual experimenters, but the effects of this constant dissembling is a pollution of the subject pool and growing cynicism among the finite number of available undergraduate experimental subjects. This is an inconvenience to Bonacich, whose work in gaming strategies is disrupted by misbelieving subjects. He argued that "the long-term advantage of a policy of no deception could be a more powerful experimental manipulation because subjects would not believe they were being deceived" (Bonacich, 1970, p. 45).

2. Since the early 1980s, institutional review boards (IRBs) have increasingly inclined toward narrow and legalistic interpretations of the consent process. Section 46.101 (b) (1)-(5) (Federal Register 8366, 1981), under which some behavioral science research has been exempted from the complexity of "full disclosure" consent routines, has been criticized as posing a significant legal risk for IRBs. Reinsch (1984) argued at length that "to forego requiring informed consent . . . is a dangerous position for an IRB to be in. . . . An analysis of Section 46.101 (b) (1)-(5) [shows that] 'most behavioral science research' cannot be safely excluded . . . and an IRB is only on safe ground exempting research when it is certain that the information cannot, in any way, be linked to the subjects" (p. 121). To underscore the practical impossibility of obtaining absolute security, Graber (1979, p. 35) noted the flaws in apparently ingenious methods suggested by the Committee on Federal Agency Evaluation Research (1975, pp. 5-21), such as destroying data as soon as is feasible, destroying information linking subjects to data, and keeping subject-linkage files in a distant place, for example, in a foreign country (called "link file brokerage"). Because none of these techniques warranties perfect separation of data from subject identities, none serves as the basis for claimed exemption under applicable federal regulations. As Reinsch (1984) concludes, "Despite the comment by HHS that most social science research is exempt, Section 46.101 is merely a trap for the unwary, because it contains many vague terms that have not been defined by any court of law" (p. 120). This is a risk Reinsch (1984) and an increasing number of IRBs consider untenable.

3. There is a serious but officially unrecognized inequity in the arbitrary code baseline against which research hazards are to be evaluated, the so-called "risks of everyday life." As Sieber (1984b, p. 40) noted, risk is typically defined from the researcher's particular technical and cultural perspective. Many well-educated, middle-class academics fail to recognize that the risks of everyday life vary from one category of persons to another. The poor, young persons, minorities, and institutionalized populations all chronically face significantly greater risks of criminal victimization, economic exploitation, and invasion of privacy than do the wealthy and powerful. Yet it is from these inequitable starting points that research-generated risk is judged. Acceptance of the unelaborated risks of everyday life as a benchmark may lead to paradoxical circumstances where, for example, an upper-level manager of a savings and loan association might claim greater absolute protection from research intrusions than an imprisoned minority youth because their risks of everyday life differ dramatically.

4. Section I-B-9 of the 1989 version of the ASA code stipulates that "study design and information gathering techniques should conform to regulations protecting the rights of human subject [sic], irrespective of source of funding, as outlined by the 'Regulations Governing Research on Human Subjects: Academic Freedom and the Institutional Review

Board' " (p. 3). This requisite is less clear than first appearances would suggest. Ambiguity arises when the AAUP document is examined. It is not, as implied, a self-contained code or set of regulations. Rather the report is a complex argument for specific revisions to the exemptions incorporated in the recommendations of the National Commission for the Protection of Human Subjects of Biomedical and Behavioral Research. The latter regulations govern researchers at institutions where work is funded by the Department of Health and Human Services.

5. As an illustration of the impracticality of some informed consent procedures, Applebaum (1984, p. 33) observed that of the instances known to him "full disclosure" consent contracts require a minimum of 1 and, in many instances, up to 3 single-spaced typewritten pages of text to detail all the applicable Department of Health and Human Services contingencies. There is evidence that these complex forms may confound rather than clarify research procedures. In a classic study, Epstein and Lasagna (1969) systematically varied the length and detail of consent forms presented to subjects. They found comprehension and frequency of consent were inversely related to the length of the forms. Cassileth et al. (1980) found that only 60% of 200 patients consenting to chemotherapy understood the purpose of the treatment when interviewed 24 hours after signing full disclosure forms. Only 55% could list one possible adverse effect of the therapy. Roth et al. (1982) identified level of formal education as central to a subject's understanding of consent forms in psychiatric research, while noting that in many studies education is unevenly distributed. It is also worth noting that in the most often cited instance of subject abuse in the social sciences, Milgram's obedience studies, participants did review and sign informed consent contracts.

6. Bond (1978, p. 146) cited eight instances of subpoenas and/or political pressures applied by grand juries, government agencies, and law enforcement to researchers. Demands were made for investigators to release data on individual subjects in cases involving studies of juvenile gang members (suspected of petty crimes), welfare recipients (suspected of fraud), persons reporting criminal victimization (suspected by local law enforcement of inflating their claims), and persons expressing attitudes toward compulsory busing. In refusing to provide these data, investigators were variously fired, imprisoned, publicly vilified, and professionally sanctioned.

7. These documents are archived and made available to interested researchers through the Manuscript Division of the Library of Congress. Although some information has undoubtedly been omitted from these records, the collection is extensive and carefully indexed and ordered in such a manner that topic-relevant sections are readily identifiable.

8. By proclaiming the inherent dangers of empirical sociology and adopting a code structurally similar to ones in the fields of medical research, sociology wraps itself in a mantle of respectability and utilitarian success of a leading branch of the natural sciences. Along with respectability comes apparent strength because, if a strong code is needed to contain and limit secret sociological research, then sociologists must possess potent tools capable of powerful results. Restrictions against secret investigations have become prerequisites for participation in the competition for limited resources from governmental and private funding agencies (see AAUP, 1981; Pattullo, 1984; Sieber, 1984b, pp. 148-149). Disciplines that incorporate the procedural requirements of these agencies into formal codes of conduct favorably position themselves in the contest for limited research funds. Such codes provide demonstrable proof of compliance and specific guidelines for individuals seeking support. Furthermore, codes that require informed consent documentation may offer partial protection to researchers, their institutions, and funding sources in the event of litigation (Gray, 1975,

p. 239; R. J. Levine, 1978, p. 3). In the report of the Consultive Group on Ethics of the Social Sciences and Humanities Research Council of Canada (1977), the advantages of written informed consent forms is made explicit: "The consent form itself is tangible evidence of an act of voluntary cooperation between researcher and his subject. . . . It is, in effect, a contract, and its purpose is the protection of both subjects and the researcher and no less the sponsoring institution" (p. 8). Such codes in themselves suggest internal order, a cohesive discipline, and a steadily compiling set of propositional laws. Thus a code serves more as a badge of professional prestige than a buffer against harm to subjects.

9. There is reason to doubt such data exist in another discipline, namely, psychology. The American Psychological Association (1988) reported that during the period 1983-1987 there had been a "striking increase in the number of people who contact the Ethics Office expressing an intent to file a complaint" (p. 564). Its most recent data indicate less than .5% of these complaints concerned research with human subjects, second in infrequency only to ethical misuse of laboratory animals. What complaints were received? Grievances concerning grades, tenure and promotion, sex, race, and age discrimination and harassment (in grades, promotion, tenure), pay scales, and benefit packages for various employees comprised most of the list.

10. It is worth noting that the first case to come before an ethics committee of the ASA was not a matter concerning abused research subjects but one regarding investigators' professional competence. Specifically, this case concerned the representativeness and interpretation of an American Medical Association (AMA)-sponsored survey of America's elderly. According to the AMA, the survey demonstrated that the nation's elderly were by and large physically well, medically well-cared for, and without the need of government assistance in their health matters (ASA Archives, 1961-1962, p. 2; Morgan, 1960, p. 11).

11. They second Haan's criticisms (1982) of those who "seem to regard moralities as revelations that the wise make for the guidance of the unwise rather than achievements made by people in their social living" (p. 1099). This outlook, she noted, is based on the "implicit assumptions [that] the common person is morally weak [and] the practical problem is to curb (or transform) the moral weakness of the populace" (pp. 1099-1100).

5. SECRECY, RISK, AND RESPONSIBILITY

Independence

How are fieldworkers to evaluate the preceding arguments? Although the liberal complaint against secrecy in research is empirically unsubstantiated, it is not without effects. Considerable formal opposition remains aligned against those who espouse and practice covert investigation. Is that disfavor sufficient justification for fieldworkers to reject liberal concerns and the institutions that support them? Some may come to that conclusion, but I would first urge activism. Fieldworkers can act constructively toward liberal opposition in several ways. Qualitative researchers should seek every opportunity for participation in those decision-making bodies defining research propriety. Institutional review boards and professional ethics oversight committees must learn from practicing fieldworkers firsthand of the ethnographer's circumstances, and they must be urged to consider these circumstances in developing and interpreting regulations. Vigilance too is required. To question codes and other institutional constraints on covert qualitative research is not to advocate careless complacency. The liberal refrain, although often overamplified, nonetheless contains essential cautionary notes. If the record of abuse of subjects by social scientists is brief, every effort should be made to keep it so. A dialogue concerning research ethics is of critical importance to development of the social sciences and fieldworkers should be active participants therein. But they should not expect rapid acceptance of their perspectives. Although responsible arguments in favor of covert research have been made since mid-century, professional codes and regulations continue toward legalism and narrowed and negative interpretations.

Institutional frameworks credential and sometimes support our work. They also may limit its scope, transform its qualities, and diminish its merits. Ultimately, ethnographers must choose their own course between the requisites of the formal organizations to which they owe allegiance and the realities of the field. Some will come to the conclusion that to practice their craft to their full capacities fieldwork must become more than a method. It must become an unencumbered, independent way of life, a direct comprehensive engagement with the social world. Such work is not for everyone. It is risky business, an uncertain, demanding, often lonely, and occasionally dangerous undertaking in which secrecy is unavoidable and ethical judgments are constantly required.

Jean Peneff's (1981, 1985) accounts of his research among postrevolutionary Algerian industrialists show the need for independent research and some of the hazards such fieldwork entails. They also illustrate the fluid and emergent nature of research roles discussed earlier and several manifestations of secrecy fieldworkers may encounter or employ. Peneff's tale sets the scene for a final consideration of fieldworkers' responsibilities to their subjects, their disciplines, and themselves.

Fieldwork in Algeria

Peneff was one of a small number of young faculty who found themselves restaffing the University of Algeria after European professionals left the country en masse in 1962. He was interested in studying emerging Algerian industrialism, an economic development academics prior to the revolution had predicted would be improbable without French help. Peneff's work progressed through three phases, each distinct in the specific research role he played, the ways others interpreted that role, and the secrets kept on both sides.

THE ACADEMIC

Knowing nothing of ethnographic methods, Peneff began his research by constructing 30-plus questions to structure the interviews he hoped to have with local businessmen. Items like "Who loaned you the money to start your business?," "What was your father's occupation, the professions of your relatives and friends?" and "What did you do before the revolution?" were the sort he planned (Peneff, 1985, p. 67). Next he obtained sponsorship and letters of introduction from his home institution, identifying him as a member (he was actually the chair) of the University of Algeria's sociology faculty. Finally, he needed a sample of businesses to investigate. For this information he turned to the Office National de la Propriete Industrielle, which provided a list of factory addresses and owners' names. Secrecy seemed neither necessary nor appropriate in these preparations, or in the work ahead. With professional credentials, university and government backing, and a seemingly noncontroversial topic of study, he anticipated no particular trouble in the field. He was wrong.

Fieldwork went poorly. In his role as an objective academic researcher, Peneff was ill-received. The industries he sought to study were not listed in telephone books or marked by streetside signs. Most, in fact, were hidden in basements, flats, and farms surrounding Algiers. This intentional conceal-ment was the result of the Algerians' traditional penchant for secrecy and also, as Peneff was to learn, more immediate reasons. Nor were people on the streets willing to help him find the businesses he sought, even when telltale chemical smells and the sounds of machinery made the presence of nearby manufacturing facilities obvious.

The problem lay in the way people interpreted Peneff's self-presenta-tion. His attempts to be clear and candid regarding his identity were taken by locals as tacit proof of his fundamental dishonesty. Unknowingly, he had come to bear "the heavy weight of sponsorship" (Peneff, 1985, p. 69). As he was to learn, in Algeria, as in other underdeveloped countries, the idea of objective academic sociology is largely meaningless. For people preoccupied with the pressure of daily subsistence, the notion that expen-ditures of time and money might be made merely for the luxury of studying social processes and structures, without ulterior motives, is nearly incom-prehensible (Peneff, 1985, p. 70). It makes more sense, at least from a Third World perspective, to interpret such researchers as representatives of the organizations that support them and their research as self-interested efforts to forward those organizations' policies. It was in this context that Peneff was being evaluated. The postrevolutionary socialist government in power in Algeria at that time was, in general terms, opposed to unregulated industry. Peneff's admitted ties to the state-owned university and his (totally out of date) government-supplied list of businesses con-firmed for most community members that he was, in fact, not the naive, neutral scholar he claimed to be. It seemed more reasonable to assume that he was both knowledgeable and unsympathetic, probably a tax collector, plainclothes police officer, or other federal agent sent to spy on them or a union organizer sent to stir up labor unrest. Not surprisingly, neither business owners nor the many unemployed Algerians who looked to the local firms for work were inclined to help Peneff in his investigations.

THE ADVOCATE

When Peneff came to realize the stigma attached to his university and government ties, he changed his strategy. He quit identifying himself as a sociologist-academic, disposed of the useless but onerous government business list, and obtained sponsorship from the Chamber of Commerce. In this new research role things went better. He was well-received by the nascent industrialists, but in time new and more sinister troubles arose. The weight of sponsorship continued to bear on him. Institutional affiliation extracted another price. His association with the Chamber of Commerce proved not to be benign. The chamber and its supporters represented a political faction favoring capitalist development. By publicly identifying himself with this faction, Peneff appeared to advocate opposition to the existing socialist government. Again the notion of disinterested social science research seemed implausible. Capitalists and socialists alike interpreted his actions in their own terms. Neither group perceived him as a naive-sympathetic outsider. Opposition leaders with whom he met judged him to be aligned with their cause and suggested he use his findings against the government by publishing critical remarks in a French journal. Government observers presumed his research was a cover for antisocialist organizing efforts. This latter misattribution was not unreasonable. At that time, French and other national agents were trafficking in Algerian currency and trying to destabilize the socialist government. Now genuine dangers arose. Peneff's home telephone was tapped. He was followed by plainclothes policemen. Members of the secret police sought to entrap him in antigovernment declarations that could have led to his imprisonment. Eventually, as these attempts at incrimination failed, government pressures were brought on the university. He was fired and forced to leave the country, his research incomplete and his career suddenly uncertain.

THE PRESTIGIOUS FOREIGNER

In time, Peneff was able to establish himself at a French university and reflect on his unfinished investigation. He decided to try again. This time he began by fabricating a fictitious biography and profession. He had phony business cards and credentials printed identifying him as a high-level sales representative of a (nonexistent) French firm selling industrial supplies and equipment in northern Africa. He dressed the part in business suits, carried the traditional briefcase and marketing papers, and entered Algeria with the declared intent of selling merchandise. Algerian agents were comfortable with the role of a visiting French businessman. Such an individual might be presumed unsympathetic to the government of France's former colony but was likely harmless. People on the streets, too, were agreeable, cooperatively showing him the way to hidden businesses. Once inside, secretaries and workers introduced him to the firm's owner. Now another ruse began. When introductions were complete, Peneff acted embarrassed and surprised. He pretended to have inadvertently come to the wrong manufacturer. If the business he was in produced food, then Peneff said he was in clothing or some other line, but he did not hurry to leave. "I showed my interest in his business and we started a discussion on various topics such as the economic situation or the international market" (Peneff, 1985, pp. 71-72). From then on his research usually went well. Peneff's research role was suited to the context in two respects. On one hand, he was seen as an important French business representative, a capitalist ally, presumably knowledgeable in modern international commerce. Consequently, his relationships with many firm owners progressed rapidly; soon he was being treated as an intimate, an insider. Businessmen shared autobiographical details of their secret activities in the underground resistance during the revolution. Peneff learned how Islamic sects concealed the true ownership of entrepreneurs' property, protecting it from French wartime appropriation. He was told of nighttime schooling in the Koran given to the children of revolutionary leaders after they attended French day classes. Peneff was taken backstage to private sporting clubs and bars where businessmen gathered for leisure. Owners confided what they said were their real profits and how these differed from figures reported to the government. On the other hand, although Peneff was viewed as a knowledgeable French businessman, he was also seen as a newcomer, young, and ostensibly unfamiliar with Algerian industrialism. He managed this apparent naivete for effect, and the entrepreneurs responded. They set out to socialize him, to align him with their causes.

> I feigned surprise—in a racist way—at finding so many Muslim industrialists. To counter this ignorance, my Muslim informants were eager to tell me their own stories. The fact that I was a foreigner, a temporary visitor, and younger than the entrepreneurs was helpful in gaining access and confidence. They wanted to educate me, to give me details on Muslim life and the Revolution. (Peneff, 1985, pp. 71-73)

Industrialists also made use of Peneff for their own purposes. Often he was asked to critique food, beverages, clothing, furniture, fashions, and other manufactured goods being produced for customers with French tastes and sensibilities. At other times he was called on to read, write, and interpret business correspondence (Peneff, 1985, p. 74).

With creativity and imagination, Peneff at last found ways of satisfying both his scholarly interests and members' expectations. However, can such work be considered responsible ethnography?

Responsibility

The risky business of independent research must be conducted responsibly. In declaring independence from institutional rules and practices, as Peneff had done, researchers exchange the heavy weight of sponsorship for an equal burden of moral obligation. The independent researcher, faced with ethical quandary, finds no safe retreat in the statutory specifics of codes. It is not good enough merely to obey the rules, to obtain institutional review board and funding agency approvals, properly complete informed consent forms, and so forth. Responsible independents hold that reducing ethics to bureaucratic details is itself morally regressive, at least in Kohlberg's (1981a, 1981b) sense, in two ways. First, it diminishes morality from principled professionalism to particularistic and often self-serving efforts to avoid punishment and other negative consequences, such as the loss of grants and professional prestige.[1] Second, formalizing morality into arbitrary rational-legal directives handed down from disciplinary elites discourages researchers from seeking to discover for themselves the moral perquisites of those they study. The independent scholar must do more. Having declared her or his freedom, the researcher is condemned, as Sartre (1953/1966) would have it, to the "incontestable consciousness of authorship" (p. 707), to the necessity of crafting a moral order simultaneously encompassing both researcher and the researched. Philosophers have long sought the guidelines by which such an ordering might be achieved (see May, 1980), but social scientists have also made applicable contributions to solving the problem. Consider sociologists' development of the concept of trust.

Durkheim (1893/1933) argued that trust provides a necessary precondition to all agreements, compacts, treaties, and other structured social realities, which presumably includes social science research. Trust is the silent partner, the conscious collective standing behind all contractual agreements. Following Schutz (1962), ethnomethodologists (Cicourel, 1974; Garfinkel, 1967, pp. 247-248) identify trust with the linguistic metaphor of et cetera clauses, unstipulated but assumed qualifications, and provisions of future action implicit in any and all forms of social interaction, however routinized, formal, or detailed. Barber (1984) integrated these traditions in *The Logic and Limits of Trust*, proposing that trust in social relationships has three manifestations: (a) the technical competency of actors, (b) the fiduciary responsibility of their actions, and (c) their commitment to maintenance of alter's constitutive, commonsense understandings of the world. Collectively, these constitute trust in responsible research relationships and may be recast as three specific questions: (a) Is the researcher scientifically capable? (b) Will she or he use those capabilities for subjects' benefits? (c) Will the researcher go about his or her work without disruptions to the subjects' existential order, their taken-for-granted realities? All this considered, what possibilities are there for obtaining these ideals in the conduct of responsible independent fieldwork, especially work as secret-filled and demanding as Peneff's?

COMPETENCE

Technique. Does the researcher know what he or she is doing? In the researcher's effort to develop trust, this is likely the first judgment members make of her or him. Is the researcher professionally capable? In the context of this volume, this question can be put more specifically: Does the researcher understand the technical business of qualitative researching? Other monographs in this series highlight the range of skills this business entails: depth interviewing; focus group management; abilities to analyze written, verbal, and visual texts; familiarity with the epistemological issues undergirding such work; and so forth. In the professional ethics of liberalism, moral science has become equated with technical competence in the form of strict adherence to methodological regimens. Could Peneff's subjects trust his scientific capability? In retrospect, probably not. By his own account, his methodological training was inappropriate to the setting he sought to investigate. Yet scientific competency is a quality difficult to judge during many phases of fieldwork.[2] Subjects are seldom provided direct evidence of researchers' technical skills. Even if researchers were to provide such evidence, members might have difficulty interpreting it. Furthermore, success in qualitative research is not merely the result of care in attending to technical details of data collection. The so-called facts do not speak for themselves but must be given voice in the ethnographers' emergent stories, metaphors, tropes, and other concocted symbology.

Expertise. What researchers often do to warrant members' trust is not directly demonstrate their competence but reassure members of their general expertise. Like Peneff, they play the parts they imagine members expect of them. Some act the "serious" scientist, emphasizing their credentials and sponsorship from prestigious institutions. Props of the trade—printed questionnaires, clipboards, name tags, identification cards, and legal-sounding release forms—reinforce such an impression. As Peneff discovered, competence is not always enough. No amount of demonstrated technical skill or apparent expertise would likely have improved his reception. Algerian businessmen and their supporters were largely disinterested in Peneff's scientific capacities, but they were keenly concerned about the purposes of his research. It was not how well Peneff was doing his job that worried them but for whom he was doing it.

FIDUCIARY TRUST

Will researchers use their capabilities to their subjects' benefit? In answering this question of fiduciary trust, benefit is defined in two ways, as economic advantage and as personal advocacy.

Economic advantage. Fiduciary trust may be expressed in terms of the advantages for profit or prestige persons might expect to realize from their participation in research relationships. In its preamble, the ASA's 1989 code makes this sort of utilitarian claim for regulated research. Investigators adhering to the code "maximize the beneficial effects that sociology may bring to humankind and minimize the harm" (p. 1). These economic benefits are presumably made possible by formalizing negotiations over valued goods. But who benefits? Liberals contend fiduciary trust is achieved by giving rational, self-serving subjects clear opportunities to weigh the merits of research participation through detailed informed consent procedures. Some humanists also define fiduciary trust in economic terms but claim that informed consent routines primarily benefit sponsors and other institutional backers. In this economic conception of trust, secrecy requires precise defining. Points of law are developed to distinguish secrets derived from information "acquired casually as a by-product of other activity," from "information acquired as a result of deliberate effort" which entails costs (Kronman, quoted in Scheppele, 1988, p. 33). Contracts entailing the former sorts of secrets are valid, whereas the latter kind are illicit. Elsewhere, considerable attention has been devoted to detailing the role of strategic secrecy in a variety of gamelike exchanges aimed at achieving resource advantages of one sort or another, as, for example, in Goffman's (1969) essay "Strategic Interaction" in his book of the same title, Scheppele's (1988) discussion of secrecy and strategy in chapter 3 of her book *Legal Secrets*, and Bok's (1988) *Secrets* (especially chaps. 10 and 11).

44

Advocacy. The economic interpretation of trust emphasizes fair and honest choice between clear options, but no more. An alternative view urges researchers to adopt an ethic of advocacy, to actively seek benefits for specific segments of the population by conducting research on their behalf in the interests of emancipation, as urged by Habermas and other critical theorists, and the nominal humanist tradition in North America. In this sense, researchers who offer subjects no more than the chance of refusing to be studied are less trustworthy than those who offer a personal commitment to the members' cause.

My early association with a local survivalist group provides an illustration. In those initial contacts, I made particular efforts to emphasize my academic impartiality. I repeatedly claimed my only interest was to find the truth about survivalism and write a book about it. I showed members another book I had written as a sample of the form this writing might take. My explanations were largely ignored, although for almost half a year of active participation, my presence seemed to be comfortably accepted. Then one Sunday afternoon, following the group's monthly potluck meeting, I was confronted by two of the group's officers. They made it clear that they distrusted my claim of professional neutrality. For them, fiduciary trust entailed more than my constant reminders that I was a researcher. They wanted to know where, and with whom, I stood.

> How do we know we can trust you to *help us*? . . . When you write up your book are you going to tell about survivalism like *you* think it is, or are you going to tell people how *we* see it? . . . We need people to wake up. They should join us, or start their own groups. You've got to tell people how it is so they can start preparing. . . . We don't show all this [survivalist technique] to people who don't care. These meetings are for people who are *really getting involved.* (fieldnotes, August 1985)

EXISTENTIAL ORDER

This survival group incident revealed that neither my ability to do social science research, at least as the members understood it, nor my competence to learn and report the facts of survivalism was at issue. I had been accepted as a reasonably capable practitioner of survivalist skills and they were convinced I had the ability to produce scholarly writings, albeit stuffy ones. The critical unspoken issue was not my knowledgeability, sociological talents, or willingness to use these on the group's behalf if bidden to do so. The problem implied by the officers' remarks was more serious. Although the officers did not say so, my reassurances of fiduciary responsibility were not enough. On the surface my interrogators were asking if I would help their cause. This was part of the problem, but not all of it. What was at stake was the most fundamental form of trust, trust in the existential order, trust that all participants in the group, including myself, shared a common intersubjective experience, an affective as well as technical commitment to survivalism. Members knew there was another possibility. As a researcher, I may have become well-informed about the group and its members while remaining personally disinterested in them, or worse, ill-disposed toward them. There was a possibility that I was playing the most disconcerting of research roles, that I was an informed-unsympathetic investigator.

Some critics of covert research see this suppression of affect as simple work, accomplished by daubing on a kind of cosmetic identity. Others confuse it with the work of a more dramatic character, the spy.

Notes

1. There are arguments among the several proponents of hierarchies of moral development and action (Haan, 1982, p. 1096) and especially criticism of Kohlberg's (1981a, 1981b) scheme and his admitted embrace of the naturalistic fallacy. However, in virtually all classification schemes, particularistic, rule-governed punishment avoidance is judged less "advanced," if that is the proper term, than is self-monitored, principled, holistic commitments to the well-being of others.

2. Similarly, researchers must trust that their informants possess technical capacities appropriate to the setting, that they command genuine members' knowledge and are capable, if not immediately willing, to communicate that knowledge unclouded by delusions or deletions.

46

6. THE MYTH OF COSMETIC IDENTITY

Researcher Versus Spy

To understand the informed-unsympathetic research role, it is important to differentiate covert researcher from the more romantic notion of spy. The opposite of full disclosure has been described as "deep cover" covert research (Fine, 1980, p. 124-25; cf. Whyte, 1979, p. 58; see also Erickson, 1967, p. 367; Punch, 1986, p. 72). Some contended that in investigations where subjects are to any degree unaware they are being studied "the position of the researcher is structurally equivalent to the undercover intelligence agent" (Fine, 1980, p. 124; see also Bulmer, 1982, pp. 4-5; Marx, 1974).[1] Structurally, perhaps researchers are, but not functionally. There are five essential differences in emphasis between espionage and covert qualitative research: (a) Spying is ideologically proactive, whereas research is ideologically naive. Spies seek to further an ideology, whereas researchers seek to understand subjects' belief systems and worldviews. (b) Spying is mission oriented, bound by time and circumstances to the achievement of specific instrumental tasks or, in long-term settings, to the acquisition of certain kinds of useful information. Research is global and ongoing, oriented to the full spectrum of meaning and actions that hosts may by their actions indicate are significant. (c) Spies assume they are morally superior to their subjects. Indeed, spying is deemed necessary because "immoral" agencies and institutions cannot be fully controlled by other means. Researchers enjoy no such certainty but are chronically sensitive to ways in which their own value systems may prejudice their observations. (d) Spy efforts are institutionally supported. Spies are backed by intermediaries and emergency-time contacts, provided background information, trained in data recognition and collection techniques, and provided the accoutrements necessary for partial transformations of persona (i.e., biographies, documents, costuming, language training, and cultural coaching). Covert fieldwork is usually done alone and, in spite of the proliferation of qualitative methods courses, usually without specific training in covert investigation. (e) Spies have expense accounts. Fieldworkers for the most part support their own research or incorporate it into other work for which they are paid. Of course these distinctions are not absolute. In retrospect, not all qualitative investigations have been unfunded, unfocused, and neutral. Factory fieldwork of the 1930s and 1940s, anthropology in the colonial era, and soul-saving rescue ethnography of the mission shelter and soup kitchen all have been conducted with specific intents, institutional support, and assumed moral prerogatives. But these are exceptional instances, not typical ones. Fieldwork and spying for the most part remain far removed in form, purpose, and presuppositions.

The Myth

Behind the imagery of the covert-researcher-as-spy is a myth of cosmetic identity, a belief that with skill it is possible to pass unnoticed among attentive strangers, shrouded from detection only by a few key items of disguise. In the movies, James Bond or Humphrey Bogart dons his dinner jacket, or trench coat and fedora, tucks his Beretta or Colt in the shoulder holster, and thus garbed blends unobtrusively into worlds of intrigue. There they both pass unnoticed until overtaken by moments of prescripted high drama. The notion that public identities are merely cosmetic facades lies at the root of these adventure tales (and much advertising). It makes good cinema but poor social science. In the movies, the full trappings of culture by which identity is marked are subsumed by a few items of clothing and indexical phrases. The right costume and a handful of clever lines are presumed sufficient to convey mastery of language and full understanding of interaction rituals. Behind their cosmetics, Bond or Bogart never doubt their accents, vocabularies, and argot or the appropriateness and timing of their dress and demeanor. Furthermore, these props and practices are treated as if they were free of genuine emotion, as instrumental only, to be assumed at will when researchers find them useful and discarded when not.

For different reasons, members and researchers alike may embrace versions of this myth. The myth may buttress the researcher's notion that he or she may seem to be a committed participant while actually remaining an objective observer: the notion that appearances are separable from being, that researchers can be value free. For members, the myth buffers against recognition of the socially constructed nature of group affiliation.

Realities

MEMBERS AND COSMETIC IDENTITY

Spying as economic predation. For members, the effects of spying are least disturbing if defined in economic terms. Such spies are said to have only instrumental effects: to diminish intergroup material advantages by revealing resource secrets to competitors or to denigrate intergroup status by disclosing members' failings to inimical outside agents and agencies. Economic spies, the most common heroes or villains of popular culture or group propaganda, are perceived as only cosmetically similar to members. They are overlooked and manage to pass for members only because their artful acting and clever costumes obscure their truly alien character. Understanding spying in this way poses a nominal hazard only, and some potential benefit, to group identity. Where the notion of out-group enemies bent on mischief is a part of group lore, as with survivalists and other marginalized groups, spying may unite members in postures of common indignation and renewed vigilance. Faith in the cosmetic myth reduces the task of detecting such spies to a technical problem, a process requiring only the discovery of errors in front work, finding flaws in their fictitious biographies, or catching them in forbidden action. In the movies, all that is required to uncover spies is to check their papers and clothing labels or query them about landmarks in the distant places they claim to know or about events in popular culture.[2] Strip away the misleading cosmetics and the economic spy's true alienness is revealed.

Spying as group fragmentation. The belief that spying is limited to economic predation, perpetrated by outsiders who are observably if not obviously different, obviates a more disconcerting alternative. The solidarity of any group depends on members' identification with a taken-for-granted intersubjective world of shared meanings and common purpose. While members search for economic spies in the guise of camouflaged outsiders, another source is possible. Spies may emerge from the ranks of members themselves, from individuals grown disaffected with group activities or aspirations. The notion of members-turned-traitors is not merely an economic problem but also a sociological one, posing a fundamental threat to group solidarity. Traitors are undistinguishable from members except in the direction and degree of their sympathies. And sympathies are not cosmetic, not discernible by attention to evidential detail. Traitors, by the very notion of their existence, potentially disrupt and destabilize collective identities. They make salient the transitory, socially constructed character of all relationships and the ongoing possibility that some members may redefine group participation on the bases of personal cost-benefit analyses rather than from commitments to a common cause. Because of this potential, members make efforts to redefine traitors, after the manner of other degradation ceremonies (Garfinkel, 1956), as having all along been fundamentally outsiders or enemies, thus recasting them as economic predators and reasserting the cosmetic identity claim.

DECEPTION RECONSIDERED

The notion of deception should be reconsidered at this point. As noted in chapter 4, social scientists in general and sociologists in particular can claim but a short list of ethical improprieties, with Milgram's investigations, *Project Camelot*, and *Tearoom Trade* serving as the most common (and usually the only) cited examples. What distinguishes these works and most other illustrations of psychosocial ethics abuse is not the demonstrable harm done, not the concrete negative accomplishments of these research projects, but the anticipatory conjecture they spawned.[3] *Project Camelot*, *Tearoom Trade*, and Milgram's work stimulated what-if concerns. What if Camelot had gone forward to aid repressive governments in suppressing dissension? What if Humphreys had revealed the identities of his homosexual subjects? What if the apparatus and circumstances of the Milgram experiment had been authentic? But none of these were the case. Camelot was stillborn, halted in its planning stage. Humphreys guarded his secrets in life, and took them with him to the grave.[4] Milgram's laboratory was an elaborate prop. Why then the continued ire over these so-called deceptive works?

Deception is indeed consequential. The discontents engendered in the research are neither trivial nor feigned. What liberals miss in these cases is not the seriousness of the circumstances but the cause. To liberals, deception in research is a violation of implied contract, a misrepresentation of proffered goods, a fiduciary failure of the economic sort (see Barber, 1984, pp. 7-25), for which researchers are entirely and willfully responsible.

In fact, these investigations and others like them are profoundly disturbing, even revulsive, not so much for what they conceal, for the knowledge subjects are denied, but for what such research dramatically reveals regarding cherished myths. Discovered deception sharply illuminates the arbitrary, ephemeral, socially constructed nature of everyday interaction. It reveals the social world as less than firmly predictable and understood, even as potentially absurd. Most important, revealed deceptions invite speculation regarding other social arrangements, and with speculation comes growing uncertainty. The motives and character of even significant others are brought to question and, in reflection, so too is the social self these others define. Trust in the existential order is forcibly disrupted.[5]

RESEARCHERS AND COSMETIC IDENTITY

For ethnographic researchers, the myth of cosmetic identity poses two problems, one trivial, the other more profound. In the first instance, researchers run the risk of seeming foolish by parading about in their own versions of the emperor's new clothes, which conceal nothing, least of all their ignorance. At other times the myth detracts from the need to confront their subjects' feeling worlds.

Problem: Faith in transparent disguise. On "Operation Aurora Borealis," our first weekend among the paramilitary variant of survivalists, Eleen and I tried to hide behind our costumes. "Bring firearms," the announcement read. "There will be compass problems, code, patrolling, ambush and counterambush, recon and scout, night perimeter ops." We called for directions and permission to attend. With trepidation and borrowed shotguns, we drove overnight across two states to the rendezvous point, an isolated clearing in heavily timbered National Forest land. At 8:30 a.m., the clearing was ringed with primer-spotted domestic pickups and four-door sedans with blackwall recaps and six-digit mileage. Men with guns—large and small caliber assault rifles, side arms, grenade launchers, submachine guns—stood about chatting and examining each other's weapons. They wore military camouflage over modest denim and polyester ready-wear. Their billed caps and the buckles of their necessarily ample belts proclaimed allegiance to brands of trucks and farm implements. We had come as covert researchers, hoping to blend in. We arrived driving a late-model, diesel-powered Peugeot station wagon and were disguised for the occasion in freshly pressed discount store duck-hunting outfits over preppy L. L. Bean pants, Patagonia jackets, and Nike trainers. Ambush maneuvers and gun play began. We learned how to whisper and creep, how to handle the weapons, and how to shoot at people. Another paradox arose. Our disguises were taken as signs of naive enthusiasm. (Who else would wear such ludicrous costumes?) We were accepted, treated with gentle respect, even praised. But we were never overlooked.

Problem: Faith in dispassionate observation. Sociologists from Durkheim to Goffman have drawn attention to the place of ritual in maintaining group identity and integrity. Even novice fieldworkers quickly learn the simplest and most routinized of these acts: the basic recognition signs, greeting forms, and other gesturing that demarcates group boundaries and distinguishes members from nonmembers, us from them. These secular mantras are frequent but ephemeral, largely substanceless, and easily mimicked. But at other intimate and important times, solidarity rituals require more than "hellos," "yeps," handshakes, and high signs. They require participation. Researchers must take a hand in the business at hand or offer parallel performance in kind. Researchers who would continue to learn must do more than affirm the action; they must contribute to it. To stand dispassionately aside at such crucial moments is to imply equivocation and thus risk exclusion from privileged activity.

Here is the crux of secrecy in fieldwork: Cosmetics offer only outward concealment. Whatever external appearances suggest, ethnographers are not hidden from themselves. To go on, researchers must wash off the final residue of positivism, the faith in a cosmetic self of fabricated affect behind which the real, dispassionate, objective self may hide. They must immerse themselves in their subjects' feeling worlds. For researchers sympathetic to those they study, such participation is nonproblematic. At worst, some might say these workers invalidate their findings by overidentification, by "going native." [6] But not all researchers share their subjects' worldviews. Some find their subjects' outlooks contrary to their own, even repugnant, and the rituals an excretion. Yet, as clearly, researcher participation remains the venue to broadened understanding and member acceptance.

Guarding patriots. Alone, 2,000 miles away from home, on the third day of the Christian Patriots Survival Conference, I volunteered for guard duty. They told us more security was needed to patrol the Mo-Ark Survival Base and protect the 400 participants from spies and infiltrators.

The Aryan Nations was there, with the Posse Comitatus, and the Ku Klux Klan. In the names of Reason and Patriotism and God, they urged repudiation of the national debt, and race revolution, economic assistance to small farmers, and genocide. Participants discussed these proposals over hot dogs and pop. Merchants sold commando knives, Bibles, powdered goats' milk, and naturopathic cures for cancer. People browsed. Dollars changed hands.

Four of us were assigned the evening gate watch. Into the dusk we directed late-arriving traffic, checked passes, and got acquainted. The

camp settled. Talk turned to traditional survivalist topics. First guns: They
slid theirs one by one from concealed holsters to be admired. "Mine's in ✎
the car," I lied. Then, because we were strangers with presumably a common cause, it was time for stories, to reconfirm our enemies and reiterate
our principles. We stood around a small campfire listening to distant
prayers and speeches drifting from the main assembly area. Our stories
went clockwise. Twelve O'Clock told of homosexuals who frequent a city
park in his home community and asked what should be done with them
in "the future." His proposal involved chains and trees and long-fused
dynamite taped to body parts. Understand these remarks. They were meant
neither as braggadocio nor excessive cruelty but as a reasoned proposal.
We all faced the "queer" problem, didn't we? And the community will
need "cleansing," won't it? In solemn agreement, we nodded our heads.
Three O'Clock reflected for moment, then proposed a utilitarian solution
involving nighttime and rifle practice. "Good idea," we mumbled support-
ively. Six O'Clock saw a ready labor source, after some veterinary
surgery. We exchanged small smiles at this notion. One more car passed
the gate. It grew quiet. It was nine o'clock. My turn. I told a story too.

As I began, a new man joined us. He listened to my idea and approved,
introduced himself, then told me things not everyone knew, about plans
being made, and action soon to be taken. He said they could use men like
me and told me to be ready to join. I took him seriously. Others did too.
He was on the FBI's "Ten Most Wanted" list. ◦

If there are researchers who can participate in such business without
feeling, I am not one of them nor do I ever hope to be. What I do hope
is someday to forget, forget those unmistakable sounds, my own voice,
my own words, telling that Nine O'Clock story.

Notes

1. Bulmer (1982) claimed that "covert participant observation is analogous to situations
in which political organizations are infiltrated by agents provocateur or spies working for
bodies hostile to that organization" (p. 4). He cited as an example the infiltration of a South
African secret police agent into the Geneva-based International University Exchange Fund,
an independent organization that provides scholarships for South African refugees. This is
hardly an instance of academics insinuating themselves into the confidences of naive
subjects. It is more nearly a case of an institution with university ties being infiltrated by a
government agent.

2. The cinematic search for spies goes something like this: The young American spy
(Captain Kraus) is being questioned by the wily World War II German officer. Officer (slyly):
Soooo, Captain Kraus, I see from your file you were at the Academy in '38. We have

something in common. I too was there briefly. I was fond of taking a glass of wine in town in the afternoons at that quiet tavern on the north end of the square beneath the handsome green clock tower. Did you perhaps visit that same tavern? American spy (cleverly): Well, no sir, I did not. As you recall there was a fire in July that burned the buildings on the south end of the square where the tavern and tower were located and they both were destroyed. But my sweetheart and I did often go to the Strauss bakery on the north end of the square for a piece of their famous strudel. Officer (satisfied): Ah, yes, you are correct. My memory is not so good these days. And in the South Pacific jungles of World War II another test takes place. A voice calls out of the dark: Hey Joe! How are you? I am a lost American soldier. I am trying to find my unit. Do not shoot. Suspicious GI in front line foxhole: Oh yea, so you are an American, huh. Tell me who pitched the fifth game of the World Series last year?

3. Project Camelot was criticized for its covert sponsorship, not fieldwork, for its "covert financing of university social science" (see Evan, 1967, p. 243), not the covert actions of the scientists involved.

4. Humphreys kept the master list of his subjects' names and code numbers in a locked box at a location only he knew, 1,000 miles from the city in which he collected data. He even went to jail rather than reveal its whereabouts. Later he destroyed the list. During and after his research the identity of his subjects was absolutely protected (Reiss, 1978, p. 175).

5. Much routine attitudinal research is also of this what-if sort. Respondents are asked to select standardized responses indicating their likely behavior if such-and-such a situation existed (a minority moved in next door, you were to vote for president, etc.). These works entail little disruption to the existential order precisely because the "behavior" manifested in standardized interviews and paper-and-pencil research is so far removed from action of consequence.

6. The problem here is not overidentification or rapport, as Miller (1953) asserted and others implied. Rather it is whether the researcher, once thoroughly enmeshed in his or her subject's worlds, will be inclined or even be able to continue the sociological task of reporting his or her experiences therein. Will the subjects' concerns and interests take such precedence that social science work dwindles to insignificance? Going native is not so much a hazard to understanding as it is a potential conflicting demand on the researcher's limited time, energy, and intellectual resources.

7. CONCLUSION

Secrecy in research is risky but necessary business. If the social sciences are to continue to provide substantive, enduring insights into human experience, timid inquiry will not do. "Take it or leave it," said Merleau-Ponty (1962). "We cannot have truth without danger" (p. 135). The personal, even physical risks of fieldwork, although infrequent, have long been familiar. Qualitative researchers have been beaten by gang members and implicated in criminal activity (Jankowski, 1991), threatened by lynch mobs (Powdermaker, 1966), tracked by secret police (Peneff, 1981, 1985), and otherwise individually assaulted, abused, and coerced. These are part of the danger to which Merleau-Ponty refers, but the lesser part. At greater risk is the worth of social science itself. To face these challenges, independent researchers need to look upward, as the humanists contend, and inward.

Technical competence is not enough. Upward are the dangers of encountering consequential people and processes objectionable to and hostile toward social science. If anxious scholars seek to avoid these encounters by overemphasizing the need to avoid secrecy for the protection of subjects, important work may go undone and weightier secrets may be kept. Behind the screen of formal ethics, timorous social scientists may excuse themselves from the risk of confronting powerful, privileged, and cohesive groups that wish to obscure their own actions and interests from public scrutiny. But they do so at the peril of their professions. If social scientists fail to explore hostile research environs, their disciplines may be diminished, homogenized by ethics routines and restrictions to the exercise of orthodox methodologies and standardized procedures, and directed into narrowed venues of application. Independent researchers face up to these challenges even when they must do so unsupported by peers, funding agencies, or professional organizations. They keep both secrets and a commitment to the humanist call for advocacy and a purpose-filled science.

Looking inward, researchers face the greatest dangers, the dangers of self-doubt and questioned identity. Secrecy, always present, is also always double-edged. The survivalists who questioned my motives (see chap. 5) were correct in their suspicions that I was keeping secrets, that I was inwardly unsympathetic to their cause and practices. I made considerable effort to repress my feelings against survivalism while with them and in other research settings. Outward appearances could be managed, up to a point, thus existential trust could be maintained. For this task, secrecy was not undesirable but essential, and I felt obliged to use it to full effect, as did Peneff, Ortiz, and others. But whereas maintaining existential trust often requires outward dissembling, the fashioning of affective fronts, and the buffering of members' sensibilities from the researcher's true sympathies, fiduciary responsibility calls for something else. To act responsibly in a fiduciary sense, researchers cannot isolate themselves from members' feeling worlds but must seek full personal immersion therein. Bergson (1912) set the most important task for independent researchers: "There are two profoundly different ways of knowing a thing," he insisted. "The first one implies that we move around the object; the second that we enter into it" (quoted in Levi, 1959, p. 66). Here is the crux of responsible social science. At risk is the potential for researchers to equivocate in this challenge and rest their ethical cases on methodological routines, while as social selves they remain outsiders, objective analysts with their own overreaching agendas. Researchers may fail fundamentally to meet the most crucial of fiduciary responsibilities, the responsibility for informed reporting of members' perspectives. They may fail to well and fully understand and report the social world as members themselves experience it. In insisting on expressive distance, in conducting work from positions of convenience, in relative power or control, researchers may achieve only incomplete understandings.

In order to understand, researchers must be more than technically competent. They must enter into cathected intimacies, open themselves to their subjects' feeling worlds, whether those worlds are congenial to them or repulsive. They must confront the duality of represented and experienced selves simultaneously, both conflicted, both real.

Here the informed researcher's voice no longer provides an authoritarian monologue but contributes a part to dialogue. At the survivalist campfire, in the Algerian factory, and wherever researchers immerse themselves in vitally lived experience, they realize they are no longer distanced from the action and the discourse but unavoidably implicated in its production. Bergson's (1912) challenge is met. The social scientist joins Camus's[1] (1942/1975) list: the artist, writer, dramatist, and other interpreters of culture who discover in these postmodern times that they are as much defined by their work as it is defined by them. Finally and fundamentally, fieldworkers understand. They can keep no secrets from themselves. In action of consequence, there is no frontier between appearing and being.

Note

1. In mind here is Camus's (1942/1975) essay on "Absurd Creation" in *The Myth of Sisyphus*, although he made the point elsewhere. Sartre concurred, as (he claimed) did Gide, that "feeling is formed by the acts one performs" (quoted in Tillman, Berofsky, & O'Connor, 1967, p. 700).

REFERENCES

Abbott, A. (1983). Professional ethics. *American Journal of Sociology, 88*, 855-885.

Adler, P. A., & Adler, P. (1987). *Membership roles in field research.* Newbury Park, CA: Sage.

Adler, P., & Adler, P. (1989, August). *Self-censorship: The politics of presenting ethnographic data.* Paper presented to American Sociological Association Annual Meetings, section on Qualitative Methodology: Old Problems Revisited, San Francisco.

Akerstrom, M. (1990). *Betrayal and betrayers: The sociology of treachery.* New Brunswick, NJ: Transaction.

American Association of University Professors. (1981). Regulations governing research on human subjects: Academic freedom and the institutional review board. *Academe, 67,* 358-370.

American Psychological Association. (1988). Trends in ethics cases, common pitfalls, and published resources. *American Psychologist, 43,* 564-572.

American Sociological Association. (1968). Toward a code of ethics for sociologists. *American Sociologist, 3,* 316-318.

American Sociological Association. (1989). *Code of ethics.* Washington, DC: Author.

American Sociological Association Archives. (1961-1962). *Matters pertaining to Committee on Professional Ethics* (Container 87, Library of Congress). Washington, DC: American Sociological Association.

American Survival Guide. (1984a, May). pp. 74-77.

American Survival Guide. (1984b, May). pp. 8-10.

American Survival Guide. (1984c, May). pp. 42-43.

Apel, K.-O. (1982). The situation of man as an ethical problem. *Zeitschrift für Pädagogik, 28,* 677-693.

Applebaum, P. S. (1984). Informed consent—Always full disclosure? In J. E. Sieber (Ed.), *NIH readings on the protection of human subjects in behavioral and social science research* (pp. 32-35). Frederick, MD: University Publications of America.

Barber, B. (1984). *The logic and limits of trust.* New Brunswick, NJ: Rutgers University Press.

Basirico, L. (1986). The art and craft fair: A new institution in the old art world. *Qualitative Sociology, 9,* 339-353.

Bergson, H. (1912). *An introduction to metaphysics* (T. E. Hulme, Trans.). London: G. P. Putnam.

Best, J. (1987). Rhetoric in claims-making: Constructing the missing children problem. *Social Problems, 34*(2), 101-117.

Best, J. (1990). *Threatened children: Rhetoric and concern about child-victims.* Chicago: University of Chicago Press.

Best, J., & Horiuchi, G. T. (1985). The razor blade in the apple: The social construction of urban legends. *Social Problems, 32,* 488-499.

Blumer, H. (1969). *Symbolic interactionism: Perspective and method.* Englewood Cliffs, NJ: Prentice-Hall.

57

58

Bok, S. (1989). *Secrets: On the ethics of concealment and revelation*. New York: Vintage. (Original work published 1983)

Bonacich, P. (1970). Deceiving subjects: The pollution of our environment. *American Sociologist, 5*, 45.

Bond, K. (1978). Confidentiality and the protection of human subjects in social science research: A report on recent developments. *American Sociologist, 13*, 144-152.

Briddell, D. W., Rimm, D. C., Coddy, G. R., Kravitz, G., Sholis, D., & Wunderlin, J. R. (1978). Effects of alcohol and cognitive set on sexual arousal to deviant stimuli. *Journal of Abnormal Psychology, 87*, 418-430.

Brown, P. (1989). Psychiatric dirty work revisited: Conflicts in servicing nonpsychiatric agencies. *Journal of Contemporary Ethnography, 18*, 183-201.

Brubaker, R. (1984). *The limits of rationality: An essay on the social and moral thought of Max Weber*. London: Allen & Unwin.

Bulmer, M. (1982). *Social research ethics: An examination of the merits of covert participant observation*. New York: Holmes and Meier.

Camus, A. (1975). *The myth of Sisyphus*. Middlesex, England: Penguin. (Original work published 1942)

Cassell, J. (1978). Risk and benefit to subjects of fieldwork. *American Sociologist, 13*, 134-143.

Cassell, J. (1980). Ethical principles for conducting fieldwork. *American Anthropologist, 82*, 28-41.

Cassileth, B. R., Zupkis, R. V., Sutton-Smith, K., & March, V. (1980). Informed consent— Why are its goals imperfectly realized? *New England Journal of Medicine, 302*, 896-900.

Castaneda, C. (1968). *The teachings of Don Juan: A Yaqui way of knowledge*. New York: Ballantine.

Cicourel, A. V. (1974). *Cognitive sociology: Language and meaning in social interaction*. New York: Free Press.

Clayton, B. (1981). Nuclear nonsense: Dispelling "doomie myths." *Survive, 1*(1), 34-37, 61-62, 64-65.

Coates, J. (1987). *Armed and dangerous: The rise of the survivalist right*. New York: Hill and Wang.

Committee on Federal Agency Evaluation Research, National Research Council. (1975). *Protecting individual privacy in evaluation research*. Washington, DC: National Academy of Sciences.

Djilas, M. (1957). *The new class*. New York: Praeger.

Dorn, D. S., & Long, G. L. (1974). Brief remarks on the association's code of ethics. *American Sociologist, 9*, 31-35.

Douglas, J. D. (1976). *Investigative social research: Individual and team field research*. Beverly Hills, CA: Sage.

Douglas, J. D., & Johnson, J. M. (1977). *Existential sociology*. Cambridge, MA: Cambridge University Press.

Douglas, J. D., Rasmussen, P. K., & Flanagan, C. A. (1977). *The nude beach*. Beverly Hills, CA: Sage.

Durkheim, E. (1933). *The division of labor in society*. New York: Free Press. (Original work published 1893)

Duster, T., Matza, D., & Wellman, D. (1979). Fieldwork and the protection of human subjects. *American Sociologist, 14*, 136-142.

59

Epstein, L. C., & Lasagna, L. (1969). Obtaining informed consent—Form or substance? *Archives of Internal Medicine, 123,* 682-688.

Erickson, K. T. (1967). A comment on disguised observation in sociology. *Social Problems, 14,* 366-373.

Evan, W. M. (1967). Report of the Committee on Professional Ethics. *American Sociologist, 2,* 242-244.

Fichter, J. H., & Kolb, W. L. (1953). Ethical limitations on sociological reporting. *American Sociological Review, 18,* 544-550.

Fine, G. A. (1980). Cracking diamonds: Observer role in little league baseball settings and the acquisition of social competence. In W. B. Shaffir, R. A. Stebbins, & A. Turowetz (Eds.), *Fieldwork experience: Qualitative approaches to social research* (pp. 117-132). New York: St. Martins Press.

Fox, K. J. (1987). Real punks and pretenders: The social organization of a counterculture. *Journal of Contemporary Ethnography, 16,* 344-370.

Galliher, J. F. (1973). The protection of human subjects: A reexamination of the professional code of ethics. *American Sociologist, 8,* 93-100.

Galliher, J. F. (1980). Social scientists' ethical responsibilities to subordinates: Looking up meekly. *Social Problems, 27,* 298-308.

Gans, H. J. (1962). *The urban villagers.* New York: Free Press.

Garfinkel, H. (1956). Conditions of successful degradation ceremonies. *American Journal of Sociology, 61,* 420-424.

Garfinkel, H. (1967). *Studies in ethnomethodology.* Englewood Cliffs: Prentice-Hall.

Goffman, E. (1961). *Asylums.* Garden City, NY: Doubleday.

Goffman, E. (1969). *Strategic interaction.* Philadelphia: University of Pennsylvania Press.

Gold, R. L. (1958). Roles in sociological field observations. *Social Forces, 36,* 217-223.

Graber, E. E. (1979). Privacy and social research. In M. L. Wax & J. Cassell (Eds.), *Federal regulations: Ethical issues and social research* (pp. 23-42). Boulder, CO: Westview, for the American Association for the Advancement of Science.

Gray, B. H. (1975). *Human subjects in medical experimentation.* New York: Wiley.

Gusfield, J. (1955). Fieldwork reciprocities in studying a social movement. *Human Organization, 14,* 29-33.

Gusfield, J. (1966). *The symbolic crusade.* Urbana: University of Illinois Press.

Gusfield, J. R. (1981). *The culture of public problems: Drinking, driving and the symbolic order.* Chicago: University of Chicago Press.

Haan, N. (1982). Can research on morality be "scientific"? *American Psychologist, 37,* 1096-1104.

Hamabata, M. M. (1986). Ethnographic boundaries: Culture, class and sexuality in Tokyo. *Qualitative Sociology, 9,* 354-371.

Hesse, M. (1980). *Revolutions and reconstructions in the philosophy of science.* Bloomington: Indiana University Press.

Hilbert, R. A. (1987). Bureaucracy as belief: Rationalization as repair: Max Weber in a post-functionalist age. *Sociological Theory, 5,* 70-86.

Hochschild, A. R. (1983). *The managed heart: The commercialization of human feeling.* Berkeley: University of California Press.

Horowitz, I. L. (1965). The life and death of Project Camelot. *Transactions, 3,* 3-7, 44-47.

Horowitz, I. L. (1967). *The rise and fall of Project Camelot: Studies in the relationship between social science and practical politics.* Cambridge, MA: MIT Press.

60

Horton, R. (1979). African traditional thought and western science. In B. R. Wilson (Ed.), *Rationality* (pp. 131-171). Oxford: Blackwell. (Original work published 1967)

Humphreys, L. (1970). *Tearoom trade: Impersonal sex in public places*. Chicago: Aldine.

Jankowski, M. S. (1991). *Islands in the street: Gangs and American urban society*. Berkeley: University of California Press.

Jarvie, I. C. (1979). Explaining cargo cults. In B. R. Wilson (Ed.), *Rationality* (pp. 50-61). Oxford: Blackwell. (Original work published 1964)

Jarvie, I. C., & Agassi, J. (1979). The problem of the rationality of magic. In B. R. Wilson (Ed.), *Rationality* (pp. 172-193). Oxford: Blackwell. (Original work published 1970)

Johnson, J. M. (1977). Behind the rational appearances: Fusion of thinking and feeling in sociological research. In J. D. Douglas & J. M. Johnson (Eds.), *Existential sociology* (pp. 201-228). Cambridge, MA: Cambridge University Press.

Jones, A. S. (1992, May 2). Information or privacy: Which prevails? *The Oregonian Saturday*, p. A4.

Katovich, M. A., & Reese, W. A. II. (1987). The regular: Full-identities and membership in an urban bar. *Journal of Contemporary Ethnography, 16*, 308-343.

Kelman, H. C. (1972). The rights of the subject in social research: An analysis in terms of relative power and legitiamcy. *American Psychologist, 27*, 989-1016.

Kelman, H. C. (1965). Manipulation of human behavior: An ethical dilemma for the social scientist. *Journal of Social Issues, 21*, 31-46.

Kelman, H. C. (1970). Deception in social research. In N. K. Denzin (Ed.), *The values of social science* (pp. 65-75). Hawthorne, NY: Aldine. (Original work published 1967)

Kelman, H. C. (1968). *Time to speak: On human values and social research*. San Francisco: Jossey-Bass.

Kleinman, S., & Copp, M. A. (1993). *Emotions and fieldwork* (Qualitative Research Methods Series, Vol. 28). Beverly Hills, CA: Sage.

Kohlberg, L. (1981a). *The philosophy of moral development: Moral stages and the idea of justice*. New York: Harper & Row.

Kohlberg, L. (1981b). *The psychology of moral development: The nature and validity of moral stages*. New York: Harper & Row.

Konrad, G., & Szelenyi, I. (1979). *The intellectuals on the road to class power*. New York: Harcourt Brace Jovanovich.

Levi, A. W. (1959). *Philosophy of the modern world*. Bloomington, IN: Indiana University Press.

Levine, D. N. (1985). *The flight from ambiguity: Essays in social and cultural theory*. Chicago: University of Chicago Press.

Levine, R. J. (1978). The role of assessment of risk-benefit criteria in the determination of the appropriateness of research involving human subjects [Appendix]. In *The Belmont report: Ethical principles and guidelines for the protection of human subjects* (Vol. 2, DHEW Publication No. OS 78-0014). Washington, DC: Department of Health Education and Welfare.

Liebow, E. (1967). *Tally's corner: A study of Negro streecorner men*. Boston: Little, Brown.

Linder, S. N. (1982). *Survivalists: The ethnography of an urban millenial cult*. Unpublished doctoral dissertation, University of California, Los Angeles, Department of Anthropology.

Lofland, J., & Lofland, L. H. (1984). *Analyzing social settings*. Belmont, CA: Wadsworth.

Love, R. L. (1989). Revised code of ethics applies to allsociologist's work settings. *Footnotes, 17*(6), 13.

61

Lowery, R. P. (1972). Towards a sociology of secrecy and security systems. *Social Problems, 8*, 437-450.

Marx, G. T. (1974). Thoughts on a neglected category of social movement participant: The agent provocateur and informant. *American Journal of Sociology, 80*, 404-405.

May, W. F. (1980). Doing ethics: The bearing of ethical theories on fieldwork. *Social Problems, 27*, 358-370.

Merleau-Ponty, M. (1962). Address presented to the Bergson Centennial, May 19, 1959. In T. Hanna (Ed.), *The Bergsonian heritage* (pp. 133-149). New York: Columbia University Press.

Meyers, E. (1982). *The chosen few: Surviving the nuclear holocaust.* South Bend, IN: And Books.

Miller, S. M. (1953. The participant observer and over rapport. *American Sociological Review, 28*, 97-99.

Mitchell, R. G., Jr. (1983). *Mountain experience: The psychology and sociology of adventure.* Chicago: University of Chicago Press.

Mitchell, R. G., Jr. (1990). An unprincipled ethic? The missing morality of the ASA code. *American Sociologist, 21*, 271-274.

Molstad, C. (1991, February). *The insider as ethnographer: Covert research roles, their advantages and limitations in work settings.* Paper presented to the 1991 Gregory Stone Symposium of the Society for the Study of Symbolic Interaction, section on Whither Ethnography? Vexatious Issues, University of California, San Francisco.

Moore, G. E. (1903). *Principia ethica.* Cambridge, England: Cambridge University Press.

Morgan, E. P. (1960, October 1). Cracks show up in AMA's portrait of healthy oldesters. *AFL-CIO News Saturday*, p. 11.

Nader, L. (1969). Up the anthropologist: Perspectives gained from studying up. In D. Hymes (Ed.), *Reinventing anthropology* (pp. 284-311). New York: Pantheon.

Nicolaus, M. (1969). Remarks at ASA convention. *American Sociologist, 4*, 154-156.

Olesen, V. (1979). Federal regulations, institutional review boards and qualitative social science research: Comments on a problematic era. In M. L. Wax & J. Cassell (Eds.), *Federal regulations: Ethical issues and social research* (pp. 103-118). Boulder, CO: Westview, for the American Association for the Advancement of Science.

Ortiz, Steven M. (1991, February). *Why should we trust you? Maintaining anonymity and confidentiality in celebrity interviewing.* Paper presented at the Society for the Study of Symbolic Interaction, Gregory Stone Memorial Symposium, University of California, San Francisco.

Ortiz, Steven M. (1992, April). *A Blumerian perspective on the implications of selective honesty in research.* Paper presented to the Pacific Sociological Association, Section on Theory, Oakland, CA.

Patrick, J. (1973). *A Glasgow gang observed.* London: Heinemann.

Pattullo, E. L. (1984). Institutional review boards and social science research: A disruptive, subjective perspective, retrospective and prospective. In J. E. Sieber (Ed.), *NIH readings on the protection of human subjects in behavioral and social science research* (pp. 10-17). Frederick, MD: University Publications of America.

Peneff, J. (1981). *Industriels Algeriens.* Paris: Editions du Centre National de la Recherche Scientifique.

Peneff, J. (1985). Fieldwork in Algeria. *Qualitative Sociology, 8*, 65-78.

Peterson, R. G. (1984). Preparing for apocalypse: Survivalist strategies. *Free Inquiry in Creative Sociology, 12*(1), 44-46.

Ponse, B. (1967). Secrecy in the lesbian world. *Urban Life, 6,* 313-338.

Powdermaker, H. (1966). *Stranger and friend: The way of an anthropologist.* New York: Norton.

Punch, M. (1986). *The politics and ethics of fieldwork.* Beverly Hills, CA: Sage.

Reinsch, R. W. (1984). Potential legal liability of IRB's: A legal perspective. In J. E. Sieber (Ed.), *NIH readings on the protection of human subjects in behavioral and social science research* (pp. 120-145). Frederick, MD: University Publications of America.

Reiss, A. J. (1978). Conditions and consequences of consent in human subject research. In K. M. Wulff (Ed.), *Regulation of scientific inquiry* (pp. 161-184). Boulder, CO: Westview, for the American Association for the Advancement of Science.

Rhoades, Lawrence J. (1981). *A history of the American Sociological Association 1905-1980.* Washington DC: American Sociological Association.

Richards, M. P. (1986). Goffman revisited: Relatives vs. administrators in nursing homes. *Qualitative Sociology, 9,* 321-338.

Rock, P. (1979). *The making of symbolic interactionism.* London: Macmillan.

Rollison, P. A. (1990). The story of Edward: The everyday geography of elderly single room occupancy hotel tenants. *Journal of Contemporary Ethnography, 19,* 188-206.

Rosenhan, D. L. (1973). On being sane in insane places. *Science, 179,* 1-9.

Rosenthal, R., & Jacobson, L. (1968). *Pygmalion in the classroom.* New York: Holt, Rinehart & Winston.

Roth, J. A. (1969). The codification of current prejudices. *American Sociologist, 4,* 159.

Roth, L. H., Lidz, C. W., Meisel, A., Soloff, P. H., Kaufman, K., Spiker, D. G., & Foster, F. G. (1982). Competency to decide about treatment or research: An overview of some empirical data. *International Journal of Law and Psychiatry, 5,* 29-50.

Sanders, N. K. (Trans.). (1960). *The epic of Gilgamesh.* New York: Penguin.

Sartre, J.-P. (1966). *Being and nothingness: An essay on phenomenological ontology* (H. Barnes, Trans.). New York: Washington Square Press. (Original work published 1953)

Scheppele, K. L. (1988). *Legal secrets: Equality and efficiency in the common law.* Chicago: University of Chicago Press.

Schier, R. F. (Ed.). (1985). *A guide to professional ethics in political science.* Washington, DC: American Political Science Association.

Schuler, E. A. (1969). Toward a code of professional ethics for sociologists: A historical note. *American Sociologist, 4,* 144-146.

Schutz, A. (1962). *Collected papers I: The problem of social reality.* The Hague: Martinus Nijhoff.

Shils, E. A. (1956). *The torment of secrecy: The background and consequences of American security policies.* Glencoe, IL: Free Press.

Sieber, Joan E. (1984a). Emerging ethical issues in social and behavioral research. In J. E. Sieber (Ed.), *NIH readings on the protection of human subjects in behavioral and social science research* (pp. 148-158). Frederick, MD: University Publications of America.

Sieber, J. E. (1984b). Informed consent and deception. In J. E. Sieber (Ed.), *NIH readings on the protection of human subjects in behavioral and social science research* (pp. 39-77). Frederick, MD: University Publications of America.

Simmel, G. (1906). The sociology of secrecy and secret societies. *American Journal of Sociology, 11,* 441-498.

Simmel, G. (1955). *Conflict*. Glencoe, IL: Free Press.

Sjoberg, G. (1983). Afterword. In W. B. Littrell, G. Sjoberg, & L. A. Zurcher (Eds.), *Bureaucracy as a social problem* (pp. 271-279). Greenwich, CT: JAI Press.

Social Sciences and Humanities Research Council of Canada. (1977). *Ethics: Report of the Consultive Group on Ethics*. Ottawa: Author.

Spector, M., & Kitsuse, J. I. (1977). *Constructing social problems*. Menlo Park, CA: Cummings.

Sutherland, A. (1975). *Gypsies: The Hidden Americans*. London: Travistock.

Thorne, B. (1980). "You still takin' notes?": Fieldwork and problems of informed consent. *Social Problems, 27*, 284-297.

Tillman, F., Berofsky, B., & O'Connor, J. (Eds.). (1967). *Introductory philosophy*. New York: Harper & Row.

Toulmin, S. E. (1958). *The uses of argument*. Cambridge, MA: Cambridge University Press.

Toulmin, S., Rieke, R., & Janik, A. (1979). *An introduction to reasoning*. New York: Macmillan.

Ullman, J. R. (1964). *The age of mountaineering*. Philadelphia: Lippincott.

van den Berghe, P. L. (1967). Research in South Africa: The story of my experiences with tyranny. In G. Sjoberg (Ed.), *Ethics, politics and social research* (pp. 183-197). Cambridge, MA: Schenkman.

Walters, B. (1989). ASA adopts a revised code of ethics. *Footnotes, 17*(3), 2.

Warwick, D. P. (1975, February). Social scientists ought to stop lying. *Psychology Today*, pp. 38, 40, 105-106.

Warwick, D. P. (1974). Who deserves protection? *American Sociologist, 9*, 158-159.

Warwick, D. P. (1980). *The teaching of ethics in the social sciences*. Hastings-on-Hudson, NY: Hastings Center.

Watley, R. (1953). Apophthegms. In *The Oxford dictionary of quotations* (2nd ed.). London: Oxford University Press.

Wax, M. L. (1977). On fieldworkers and those exposed to fieldwork: Federal regulations and moral issues. *Human Organization, 36*, 321-327.

Wax, M. L. (1980). Paradoxes of "consent" to the practice of fieldwork. *Social Problems, 27*, 272-283.

Wax, R. H. (1971). *Doing fieldwork: Warnings and advice*. Chicago: University of Chicago Press.

Weber, M. (1968). *Economy and society*. New York: Bedminster.

Whyte, W. F. (1979). On making the most of participant observation. *American Sociologist, 14*, 56-66.

Wilkins, L. T. (1979). Human subjects: Whose subject? In C. B. Klockars & F. W. O'Connor (Eds.), *Deviance and decency* (pp. 99-123). Beverly Hills, CA: Sage.

Winch, P. (1979). Understanding a primitive society. In B. R. Wilson (Ed.), *Rationality* (pp. 78-111). Oxford: Blackwell. (Original work published 1964)

ABOUT THE AUTHOR

RICHARD G. MITCHELL, JR., earned his M.A. and Ph.D. from the University of Southern California. He is an Associate Professor of Sociology at Oregon State University with principal research interests in interpretive studies of leisure, culture, and the sociology of sociology. His recent fieldwork has been among members of supremacist, separatist, and millennial social movements. He is the author of a dozen journal articles, numerous pedagogical publications, and *Mountain Experience: The Psychology and Sociology of Adventure* (University of Chicago Press, 1983).